The
Garland
CLASSICS OF
FILM LITERATURE

REPRINTED IN PHOTO-FACSIMILE
IN 32 VOLUMES

THE MIGHTY BARNUM

Gene Fowler
and
Bess Meredyth

GARLAND PUBLISHING, INC. ● NEW YORK & LONDON ● 1978

Copyright, 1934, by
Twentieth Century Pictures, Inc.
Hollywood, California

Library of Congress Cataloging in Publication Data

Fowler, Gene, 1890-1960.
    The mighty Barnum.

    (The Garland classics of film literature ; 9)
    Reprint of the 1934 ed. published by Covici-Friede,
New York.
    1. Barnum, Phineas Taylor, 1810-1891--Drama.
I. Meredyth, Bess, joint author. II. Title. III. Se-
ries.
PS3511.093M5 1977   811'.5'2   76-52100
ISBN 0-8240-2873-2

Printed in the United States of America

THE MIGHTY BARNUM

THE MIGHTY
BARNUM

A SCREEN PLAY

by Gene Fowler
and Bess Meredyth

COVICI · FRIEDE
NEW YORK

PHOTOPLAY RELEASED THROUGH UNITED ARTISTS

MANUFACTURED IN THE UNITED STATES OF AMERICA BY THE VAN
REES PRESS. TYPOGRAPHY AND FORMAT FOR THE SCREEN PLAY
ESPECIALLY DESIGNED BY WERNER HELMER

TO MARK KELLY
America's Sweetheart

CAST

PHINEAS T. BARNUM..............Wallace Beery

MR. B. WALSH...................Adolphe Menjou

NANCY, Barnum's Wife..............Janet Beecher

ELLEN, Barnum's Ward............Rochelle Hudson

LEANDER P. SKIFF.................John Hyams

JENNY LIND.....................Virginia Bruce

TOD, A Publicity Man..............Tammany Young

GENERAL TOM THUMB............George Brasno

LAVINIA, His Wife...................Olive Brasno

MADAME ZORRO, The Bearded Lady......May Boley

JOSIE HEATH, An Aged Negress......Lucille LaVerne

CARDIFF GIANT..............R. E. "Tex" Madsen

SWEDISH CONSUL.....................Ian Wolfe

MAÎTRE D'HÔTEL.................Charles Judels

FROG MAN.........................Herman Bing

James Gordon Greeley, Editor of the *Globe;* Mrs. Wendell-Wendell, Mrs. Waldo Astor, Mr. Waldo Astor, Mrs. Rhine-lander-Fish, New York Social Leaders; Daniel Webster; Mayor of New York, Ole, the masseur, Freaks, Carnival Crowds, Museum Attendants, Henchmen, Servants, etc.

STAFF CREDITS

JOSEPH M. SCHENCK, *President*
DARRYL F. ZANUCK, *Vice President and in Charge of Production*
WILLIAM GOETZ, *Vice President and Associate Producer*
RAYMOND GRIFFITH, *Associate Producer*
WILLIAM DOVER, *Executive Assistant to Darryl F. Zanuck*
Director: WALTER LANG
Screen Play by: GENE FOWLER and BESS MEREDYTH
HOWARD SMITH, *Scenario Editor*
Photographed by: PEVERELL MARLEY
RICHARD DAY, *Art Director*
ALFRED NEWMAN, *Musical Director*
ALLEN MCNEIL, *Film Editor*
Costumes Designed by: OMAR KIAM
HARRY BRAND, *Director of Publicity*

Production Manager.....................Edward Ebele
Assistant Director...........................Fred Fox
Still Cameraman....................Kenneth Alexander
Technical Advisor......................Ed. P. Lambert
Second Cameraman.......................Harry Davis
Set Dresser...............................Julie Heron
Assistant Cameraman....................Red Crawford
Second Assistant Director..................Charles Hall
Men's Wardrobe...................William Bridgehouse
Women's Wardrobe........................Peg O'Neil
Casting ....Bobby Webb
Scenario Secretary...................Madalin Parkinson
Scenario Secretary........................Ellen Boyer

Script Clerk..........................Marie Halvey
Makeup ....Guy Pierce
Hairdresser ....Loretta Francel
Sound Mixer..........................Frank Maher
Boom Man.............................Stan Cooley
Stage Man.............................Jack Noyes
Grip ....Buzz Gibson
Props ....M. Hershey
Gaffer ....Lou Johnson

FOREWORD

On the hot September morning when this preface is being written, Director Walter Lang is shooting the opening scene of *The Mighty Barnum*. Outside Stage 4 of the United Artists' studio, a carriage of the 1835 period is rolling along the concrete pavement. The bay horses and black vehicle draw up beside the bungalow where Mr. Eddie Cantor's 1935 automobile is parked. The coachman and chauffeur converse near a green sign, a painted board cut to simulate a clover-leaf, and which warns scenarists and other stooges to keep off Mr. Sam Goldwyn's grass.

On Stage 4 Mr. Wallace Beery, in the rôle of Barnum, is learning his lines. He wears sideburns and a merchant's apron. He perspires, partly because of the hot weather and partly because he is having a tussle with his verses. Once Beery has absorbed his lines, however, the hefty veteran can be relied upon to endow his work with something more valuable than a parrot's memory, something more interpretative than thought-up grimaces of a Hollywood automaton.

The presence on the set of a barrel of smoked fish and two tubs of redolent dill pickles is of little inspirational assistance to Mr. Beery. He labors over his script book in a manner that suggests Theodore Dreiser trying to unmix a metaphor.

Mr. Darryl Zanuck, the producer of this picture, is hopscotching up and down the concrete pavement. He even invades Brother Goldwyn's sacred sward. He scents a commercial success in this picture. Mr. Zanuck wears a yellow polo shirt and carries a long cigar as though it were a mallet. This sprightly gentleman is recently returned from Africa, where he riddled an elephant, cut down a rhino, shot a water buffalo in the eye and extinguished a family of melancholy gnus. The bouncing Mr. Zanuck is talking with Adolphe Menjou, who has been growing a House of David beard for the opening sequence of *The Mighty Barnum*. Mr. Menjou is too polite to say so, but it is believed he hopes Mr. Zanuck will break a leg so that he will quit charging around and about, getting everyone out of wind.

Amid the excitement that customarily accompanies Mr. Zanuck, at work or at play, it is impracticable for anyone to write a preface concerning the art of the cinema in general or the significance (or lack of it) of *The Mighty Barnum*. Nor does one wish to comment on art at all when one's life-long belief is that real art is expressed only in two ways—the bearing of a child or the building of a house. We are left, then, with three sentences of comment and explanation: This scenario of *The Mighty Barnum* is the first shooting script to be published in book form and pretends to function wholly inside its own medium—that of motion-picture entertainment. It violates most of the canons of literature and kicks history squarely in the groin. It seeks to create and sustain a mood in consonance with an era of pioneer showmanship.

Whenever one thinks highly of his own ability as a writer or an actor, let him visit any of the sets which are built for Hollywood productions. He will come away with a somewhat sad conviction that here, among the designers, the set dressers and the builders, is exemplified the only honesty Hollywood knows.

No billboards proclaim the genius of the creators of Hollywood scenery. Their names are not emblazoned on great screens. Crowds at the village restaurants do not ask for their autographs. Those men and women give no press interviews, and ask for none. Yet in the tiddleywinks world of celluloid people and amid the cries of drooling censors who sleep on dunghills and consort with French postcards, these forthright artisans stand as something tangible, real and constructive. Their work is reasonably free from politics, untouched by bigotry, independent of the nigger-rich snobbery of the cinematic potentates and of the monkey business of smokehouse Othellos and constipated Ophelias of Beverly Hills. They work with fidelity, speed and agility. A writer can say, with one royal belch, that such-and-such scene is to be built. A designer of that set, however, must create it with thorough understanding and despatch. His product must be built, not belched. The creator of a motion-picture set, and the one who "dresses" it, must do his or her work so well that *no one will notice it.* This fact alone conspires to keep the labors of these people anonymous. There must be a fine balance, a superb restraint in the physical creation of a background. A set must be a caricature, but of such nice delineation that it will not pass into the absurd, dominate the character of the players or impede the action of the drama. The scene must be authentic—much more so than the lines of the play. By means of a set, an audience must be able to feel the characters of the people who perform against its walls.

In launching scenic work on *The Mighty Barnum,* Art Director Richard Day began to function within ten minutes after he had received the completed manuscript. He sent his fifty research and technical aides fan-wise through the field. The period which this picture is presumed to portray is one of the most difficult for a scenic architect to recapture. From 1830 to 1855, there is a misty uncertainty concerning the realities of American life, manners, art and letters. Director Day began his research with an examination of the newspapers and periodicals of Barnum's era. It is true that the opinions of a daily press are usually hasty, inaccurate and prejudiced—Lincoln was a scoundrel, if one were to rest upon editorials that harassed him—but the life of the American people is nowhere reflected with such virile fidelity as in the news columns of its journals. Mr. Day undertook to depict the general milieu of 1835-1845, as well as the environment of a family. In all these sets, overdone as they intentionally were, Mr. Day kept within an arbitrary pattern.

The hardest set for Day to compose was Barnum's Oriental villa, "Iranistan." The authors had passed this scene along for a "glass shot," thinking it nothing more than a trick manipulation of a camera together with a painting on glass to achieve the effect. Day's problem, however, was to make an "Iranistan" background which would not utterly engulf the action—for the original picture of Barnum's villa shows it to have been unbelievably garish and rococo. The scene must not intrude. It must be in bad taste, yet not over-cluttered.

Once the blue prints were done, that unsung army of five hundred manual workers began to erect the sets. They labored in three shifts of six hours each—these expert carpenters, painters, plasterers, plumbers, mill men and electricians. They are not hit-or-miss laborers, but expert in every movement. Their work must be done swiftly and well. They are Hollywood's real poets.

Once the sets were up, the dresser, Miss Julie Heron, arrived to place furniture, pictures, curtains, pots, pans, harness, groceries, scales, churns, farm implements, wall mottoes and other paraphernalia in the Barnum ménage. Miss Heron brought twenty years of experience with her. From pins to animals, she had to procure for *The Mighty Barnum* all manner of properties. She, too, must keep within a pattern and within a mood. Her rooms seem to have been lived in by the characters playing the various rôles. Hers is a prodigious memory. She takes no notes. She reads a script and *remembers*.

The resourcefulness of all these scenic people is amazing. They can create jungles or terraced landscapes by means of rather homely articles. When birch trees are needed, rolls of toilet paper are made into a column, the wrappers charred to give the curling birch bark appearance, and then painted. Barrels, end on end, are the foundation of great tree trunks. Uncooked corn flakes are the best of photographic snow. Rubber cement blown by a two-bladed fan becomes cobwebs. Unknown beyond the Hollywood world of their own craftsmanship, these anonymous poets of the set have one advantage. When pompous writers have become valets and the strutting mimes fall upon their own thespic cans, when Tomorrow comes with its relentless amnesia, the honest and able workmen who build the scenes remain, still working, still capable, albeit still unsung.

GENE FOWLER,
Hollywood, September 17, 1934.

There is a cascade of circus music—the circus band and calliope—main title over background:

"No one book, no single photoplay ever could do justice to the mighty Barnum or depict literally the countless stirring incidents that crowded his long and fantastic career. No other saga in the annals of America's pioneers could hope to parallel the colorful legend of this master showman. No modern historian could expect to recapture ALL *the greatness of this prodigious character, a Connecticut Yankee with amazing dreams and the heart of a child, a self-styled 'Prince of Humbugs,' whose carnival drums are still heard 'round the world."*

DISSOLVE TO :

I   EXTERIOR: Circus Tents – Long Shot – Day

Under the large title: "1935." Showing crowds pouring into the tents. This is followed by QUICK DISSOLVES of the calliope; the animal tent, showing children feeding the elephants; a SHOT of trapeze artists flying through the air; a barker outside the side show; a bareback rider; and, finally, a clown riding around the hippodrome track inside the tent, seated in a small fire

17

wagon on which a gong is *clanging, clanging, clanging.*

DISSOLVE THROUGH TO:

2   CLOSEUP: A Gong

On the bow of a horse car. The gong strikes two or three times. PULL CAMERA BACK to get the lettered sign on exterior of the horse car—"New York and Harlem Street Car Company," and the date painted under it— "1835."

PAN UP to show the uniformed driver whanging the gong as he operates the horse-pulled car.

(NOTE: The New York and Harlem, the first street railway in the world, was chartered in 1831, and in 1832 opened its entire line from Prince Street to Harlem Bridge. The cars were like stage coaches, balanced on leather springs, and each had three compartments, with side doors, while overhead sat the driver moving the brakes with his feet.)

CUT TO:

3   INTERIOR: Horse Car – Reverse Shot – Driver – Shooting from behind Him

To show the two sturdy horses he is driving. We see the New York downtown street, from his angle, the single track in front of him. The traction steeds are jogging steadily along. There are a few citizens dressed in the costume of the time, moving along the

18

thoroughfare. A couple of carriages pass. There is a storm brewing, distant thunder and lightning. The driver cracks his whip to scatter some pigs from the right-of-way.

Standing beside the track, is a thin, gaunt woman, holding up a lunch pail. The driver pulls up, as he greets the hollow-eyed wench.

GAUNT WOMAN *to the driver:* Drop Louie's lunch off at the Iron Works, will yuh? *As the driver obligingly takes the pail:* ... And don't steal the pie THIS time.

---

4   INTERIOR: Horse-Drawn Car

Showing a few amusing types, including a glassy-eyed drunk, but concentrating on one man with Dundrearies. He is clasping a glass jar, partially wrapped about with paper. The car has started again, gong ringing and whip cracking bravely. The horses are non-committal —a pair of labor-hardened cynics.

MAN *holding glass jar—addressing the driver:*

Hey! Lemme off at Barnum's General Store. . . . As he speaks, he starts to his feet, clasping the precious glass jar. We do not see what is in the jar, but as the gentleman re-arranges its wrapping paper, the neighboring drunk has a peep and gives it a horrified "double-take-'em."

CUT TO:

5   EXTERIOR: Street – Shooting toward Side of
    Horse-Drawn Car

The horse car just comes to a halt, as the gentleman
with the glass jar alights from the vehicle. A few drops
of rain are falling. There are more thunder claps. The
man surveys the threatening sky.

6   EXTERIOR: Street – Follow Shot

Of the man with glass jar, as he crosses the street to
the opposite curb and steps up on the sidewalk.
CAMERA CONTINUES TO PULL BACK, DISSOLVING
THROUGH glass-paneled door of the Barnum establishment. This keeps our man in the CAMERA all the time.
As he opens the door of the shop, he looks up apprehensively at a lightning flash, and bolts in from the
gathering storm. The action of opening the door causes
the bell to jangle.

7   INTERIOR: Barnum's General Store

A picturesquely jumbled establishment, carrying everything from hardware to foodstuffs. There are several
bridles and bits hung on the wall, also some lightning
rods. A large iron stove stands in the center of the
shop. At the back is a counter, while on one entire side

are shelves filled with mysterious-looking bottles and cases. There is also a short stairway—about five steps —at the back and leading up to a closed door. Behind this door, the inside stairway continues up to the Barnums' living quarters.

In this first ANGLE SHOT (SHOOTING FROM THE DOOR), the bell is still jangling. The girl behind the counter looks up. She is about sixteen years old, but appears younger because of the child-like contour of her face. She wears a plain dress, her hair is in braids, and she is chewing on a pencil as she leans over the counter, studying a paper full of figures, trying to balance the accounts.

This is ELLEN, who lives with the Barnums. Whether or not she is their niece is beside the point. She calls Barnum "Uncle Phineas," and Mrs. Barnum "Aunt Nancy." The man with the jar advances to the counter.

 MAN *dropping his voice to a mysterious whisper:*
 Mr. Barnum around? . . .

Ellen sizes him up wisely.

 ELLEN *calling off:* Uncle Phineas. . . .

No answer.

CAMERA ZOOMS ACROSS to other side of store where the shelves are filled with mysterious bottles and cases. There are several packing boxes which have obstructed Barnum from sight. He is leaning over, his head almost to the floor, as he examines, then wrestles with, a huge and heavy bottle, so our first sight of him is a rear-end view.

ELLEN'S VOICE *on* SOUND TRACK: Uncle
Phineas!

Between the sturdy legs of Barnum, appears his head,
his face, naturally, in an upside down position. He is
puffing like a run-down moose, and as he gives a lusty
lift, his pants rip at the hips.

BARNUM: Ellie, you know better'n holler at me
when . . .

His expression suddenly changes as he sees the
stranger. He straightens up quickly and turns, his
face lighting, his attitude that of a bloodhound on the
scent.

---

8   INTERIOR: Barnum's Store — Another Angle

Including Barnum, the stranger and Ellen. Barnum's
eyes are focused on the glass jar which the man clasps
in his arms.

MAN: Could I speak with you, Mr. Barnum?

He casts a mysterious, meaningful glance at Ellen.
Barnum nods, reaches for some crackers in a jar
near by, starts chewing on them with an affected, casual
air as he turns to Ellen.

BARNUM *guilelessly, as he sniffs the air—addressing Ellen:* Smell the cabbage? *To the
stranger:* My wife cooks the best New England
boiled dinner you ever seed. *To Ellen:* Run up,
Ellie, and tell her to make some dumplin's.

22

ELLEN: She always makes dumplings, Uncle Phineas.

Barnum coughs nervously, sputters the cracker crumbs, then with the triumphant air of one who cannot be gainsaid—

BARNUM: Then tell her to make more!

Ellen realizes what he is driving at, and, with a little smile, nods demurely.

ELLEN: Yes, Uncle Phineas. . . .

He winks at her as she starts up the stairs and closes the door behind her. Both men watch until she is out of sight. Then Barnum furtively moves to the outer door, slips the bolt in place, returns to the man who has put down the glass jar on the counter and is taking off the wrappings.

MAN: Mr. Barnum, I read your ad in Mr. Greeley's paper—the *Globe*.

Barnum shoots a sly, almost harassed glance toward the door leading to the upstairs quarters. He makes shushing gestures.

BARNUM: Whatcha got, mister?

The stranger unveils his jar. Barnum peers into it.

CUT TO:

---

9   CLOSE SHOT: Glass Jar

Showing Barnum's phiz on opposite side of the receptacle. Inside the jar in the f.g. is a frog preserved in

23

alcohol. It has three heads. Barnum's pate zooms like an Assyrian sunrise above the jar, his eyes bulging.

BARNUM *with covetous passion:* Jumping Jehosophat! Where'd yah find THIS?

---

10   INTERIOR: Barnum's Store – Barnum and the Man with Frog – Close Shot

---

MAN: On my farm near Greenwich Village. Ain't often you capture a three-headed frog.

BARNUM *hovering over the jar and stroking it:* Once in a lifetime, mister. *He becomes the busy trader:* How much?

MAN: I been offered thirty dollars....

BARNUM *with a pooh-pooh air:* Talk sense, sir. I'll give you ten dollars' worth of merchandise. *With a flourish:* Look around. Anything up to THAT price in the store. Sold?

MAN *picking up some lightning rods:* I'll take twenty dollars in trade and ... *indicating rods* ... these lightning rods for my barn.

BARNUM *startled beyond repair:* Don't be insane! Why them lightnin' rods is relics. Made by their inventor, Benjamin Franklin.

MAN *reaching for his jar:* I'll take the frog to somebody that appreciates it.

BARNUM *his back to the wall:* But them rods is historic. The City of Philadelphia would give its

24

right eye to own 'em—

MAN: Let it have 'em.

BARNUM *groaning:* It's plain robbery, sir. Why don't you ast me for my coat and pants? ... *realizes for the first time his pants are torn—his shirt and underclothes are sticking out of the hole. Covered with confusion, he coughs.* We'll dismiss that last proposition, sir.

CUT TO:

---

11   INTERIOR: Kitchen on Upper Floor—Barnum's Living Quarters

---

It is a small but scrupulously clean kitchen, with shining pans hanging on the wall.

Nancy, Barnum's wife—a woman of about his own age —is preparing the New England boiled dinner. Nancy is a long-suffering wife. Migrating from Connecticut with her husband, who had a "hankering" for New York, they had invested all in this little business, aided by Nancy's father. Nancy loathes New York, and her great dream is to get Barnum to return to the small town in Connecticut, but she is trying to make the best of things.

Nancy has just finished slicing an onion into the boiling concoction on the stove, and moves swiftly across the kitchen to the cupboard to take out some dried sage from a jar. As she stands reaching for the sage, her eyes go to the half-opened door of the dining-room.

25

A rather flea-bitten cat stalks about the premises in this and other domestic scenes, at the convenience of our able director. We hope Herr Director will be a man kindly disposed to animals—and vice versa.

12   INTERIOR: Dining-Room of Barnum's Living Quarters

SHOOTING THROUGH half-opened door from kitchen. Ellen is seated on a couch at one side of the dining-room, reading a book. Nancy comes into scene.

> NANCY: Why aren't you down in the store? What's Phineas doing?

Ellen starts to answer confusedly, but Nancy overrides her.

> NANCY *continuing:* Ellen, did he send you up here to get you out of the way?
>
> ELLEN *rising lamely to Phineas' defense:* There really wasn't anything to do; he—
>
> NANCY *interrupting:* Ellen Saunders! Thou shalt not bear false witness....

CUT TO:

13   INTERIOR: Barnum's Store—Medium Shot—Barnum and Man with Frog

The tremendous business venture is concluded. The stranger is laden with groceries, and we see Barnum reluctantly placing a pair of Benjamin Franklin's lightning rods under the stranger's armpit. Barnum is sweating from commercial oratory.

BARNUM: You drive a hard bargain, sir. Them rods is wuth their weight in gold.

MAN: *getting under sail:* If I find any more monstrosities, I'll. . . .

At this moment, Barnum hears Nancy's step on the stairs. He is in a dither.

NANCY'S VOICE *on* SOUND TRACK *calling:* Phine-e-e-as. . . .

Mr. Barnum, shushing and pushing, hustles the stranger to the door and opens it as Nancy looms on the stairway landing. She looks down suspiciously.

BARNUM *to the stranger, but for Nancy's benefit:* Thanks for your generous patronage, sir. Call again. . . .

He turns back in the store, expresses surprise at seeing Nancy, and indicates the man with a jerk of his thumb.

BARNUM *continuing—pointing and winking with self-satisfaction:* Good customer. . . .

NANCY *coming down the stairs:* Did he give cash?

BARNUM *nauseated but righteous:* Why, honey, what else WOULD he give?

NANCY *slightly relieved:* Well, Phineas, you're always trading our stock for something sad and horrible.

BARNUM *rallying to the defense of his nutty pos-*

27

sessions: There you go. Them jars is wuth their weight in gold. *Nancy grunts.* You might be patient till the tide turns.

NANCY: Patient! That's all I ever been. You tore me away from Connecticut, from my father's home where I had friends and self-respect. Now look at me. Six months in New York and the wife of a snake catcher. *Sniffling and wailing:* Let's sell out and go back to Connecticut. Won't you, Phineas?

BARNUM *placating her and patting her heaving shoulder:* Don't get yourself in a tizzie, honey. We'll go back—some day. *Begins to paint a grand canvas:* We'll drive right up to your papa's door —much as I don't like him. There'll be a carriage of shiny black. Hosses. Four of 'em. White hosses with gold chains. Bands of loud music. You'll have on a shiny, black satin dress, and...

NANCY *her sobs setting in afresh:* And me in a coffin inside the hearse.

BARNUM: That's awful pestymistick after me jest makin' a big cash sale. ... *He starts away from her, and she sees the hole in his pants.* Everything's gonna be great, Nancy.

NANCY *gazing at the rent in the trousers:* You're all ripped again. ... *Shaking her head—fondly:* Won't you EVER grow up, Phineas? *Catches sight of the jar containing the three-headed frog. Is all suspicion again:* What's in that jug, Mr. Barnum?

BARNUM *scenting trouble:* What? Oh, THAT! *He moves to screen it—then becomes casual:* Just pickles.

NANCY *through her teeth:* Don't lie. It's some slimy reptile!

BARNUM *reduced to wheedling:* Why, honey, do I ever keep secrets from you?

During this scene, there have been a couple of crashes of thunder. At this point, there is a terrific clap, on top of which the bell jangles, the door bursts open, and the dripping and frenzied, apoplectic stranger bursts in.

BARNUM *aghast:* Has something happened, sir?

MAN *hoarsely:* Happened! I got struck by lightning, you cheap murderer! You robber! *He hurls the lightning rods at Barnum.*

NANCY: What's all these goings-on?

MAN: Gimme back my frog, or . . .

BARNUM: I beg you to relax.

MAN *broken speech:* . . . or ten dollars. *He begins yammering:* Police! Fake!

BARNUM *taking money from his pocket—proffering it to the stranger:* We're an honest concern.

NANCY: Why should you give him ten dollars, Phineas? Those lightning rods sell for fifty cents.

MAN: You cow-faced impostor! A lot of wormy groceries and something to kill me with! I want my three-headed frog back.

BARNUM *a heckled citizen:* Sir. . . .

NANCY *stepping into the breach:* Get out of

29

here! Whatever bargain you made with my hus-
band, YOU were sure to get the best of it! *She gives
Barnum a significant look and he wilts.*
MAN: He's a snake in the grass!
NANCY *turns her guns again on the stranger.
She advances on him:* Get out! Or I'll pull your
whiskers loose.

The stranger is abashed and leaves.

CUT TO:

---

14   EXTERIOR: Front Door Barnum's Store

Just as the stranger starts out, a charming but tipsy
young gentleman is about to enter. This worthy is Mr.
B. WALSH. He has a Blue-Book air about him but is
frayed, needs a shave and is the portrait of a well-bred
man on the down grade. It is unavoidable that he and
the fleeing stranger collide. This happens and the stranger is hurled to the walk.

WALSH *with alcoholic dignity:* My fault, sir ...
three dozen apologies. *Continuing—he reaches to
assist the fallen man:* May I lend a hand?
MAN: Lemme alone, you drunken sot!
WALSH *with a lifted brow:* Might I remind you,
sir, it was YOU who fell—not I. You will note
that MY equilibrium is beyond reproach.

He starts into the shop, staggering, but bravely bracing
himself to walk straight.

CUT TO:

30

15   INTERIOR: Barnum's Store

SHOWING back part of the store. Nancy, with Barnum
following after, is just starting up the stairs, her head
held high. Barnum is expostulating.

BARNUM *as Nancy opens the door:* Why are all
you women so unreasonable?

WALSH'S VOICE *interrupting — on* SOUND
TRACK: Their greatest charm, Phineas....

Nancy bridles as she hears this voice, but Barnum
beams.

CUT TO:

16   INTERIOR: Barnum's Store – Another Angle
Including Barnum, Walsh and Nancy

BARNUM *is batty about Mr. Walsh, and almost runs down the stairs:* Oh, Mr. Walsh!
Pumping his hand: So glad! So glad!

WALSH *to Nancy:* My profound greetings to
you, Mrs. Barnum.

NANCY *pointedly, and ignoring Walsh's greeting:* Supper's ready, Phineas.

BARNUM *between two fires:* Perhaps Mr. Walsh
would join us?

Nancy glares at her husband and flounces through the
door, slamming it. Barnum smiles and alibis the slamming door.

31

BARNUM: Nervous headache. . . . Sit down, Mr. Walsh. So glad. *He pushes out a chair for Walsh, who is weaving:* Lemme get you a seegar. *He produces a box of cigars from stock. He confides beamingly:* I've had a stroke of luck. *Looking at the living-quarters door uneasily.* Wait'll you see it.

CUT TO:

---

17   INTERIOR: Dining Room—Barnum's Living Quarters

Ellen has finished setting the table.

ELLEN *calling out to the kitchen:* Ready to dish up, Aunt Nancy?

There is no response, and Ellen starts out to the kitchen.

CUT TO:

---

18   INTERIOR: Kitchen—Barnum's Living Quarters

Nancy is sitting in a chair facing the window, her back to the dining-room door. Her head is bent over in her hands. Ellen comes up to her, puts her hand on her shoulder, knowing what ails the lady.

ELLEN: Don't be too hard on Uncle Phineas.

NANCY *there are tears in her eyes—as she grunts:* Huh? You mean too soft. The Phineas T. Barnum I married in Connecticut used to preach

32

Darryl Zanuck, producer of "The Mighty Barnum."

against demon rum. Look at him now. The consort of drunkards.

ELLEN: But Uncle Phineas never drinks. He's a teetotaler.

NANCY: His friends ain't. Look at how he runs and wheedles after that no-good, highfalutin' ...

ELLEN *catching her breath:* Is Mr. Walsh downstairs?

NANCY: Ain't he ALWAYS here? The gutter buzzard!

ELLEN *in defense of an idol:* He's not a buzzard, Aunt Nancy. He's ... he's well bred and ...

NANCY: So are my father's hogs.

ELLEN: Uncle Phineas says he has brains.

NANCY: He ain't got enough brains to make a sofa pillow for a flea.

ELLEN: Then how could he of been a professor? And write pieces for the *Globe?*

NANCY: He got thrown out of both jobs. On his hips. *She gets to her feet:* He's to blame for keeping us in a sinful city. Flattering Phineas, hypnotizing him. ... It's wicked to say, but I wish something TERRIBLE would happen to that sot. ...

ELLEN *gasping:* Don't say THAT, Aunt Nancy. *She runs from the room:* Please don't.

Nancy stares after her, as though the girl had gone daffy. Then she turns to the stove and sniffles over the soup pot.

CUT TO:

33

Walsh is tilted back on the chair, smiling sardonically.

WALSH *pointing with his cigar to the shelves:* And what do you propose to do with all these charming doodads, Phineas?

BARNUM *with a religious awe:* Open a MUSEUM.

Walsh has pulled a bottle from his pocket, takes most of what remains at one fell gulp. Barnum looks at him uneasily.

BARNUM *continuing:* Couldn't you do without THAT, Mr. Walsh?

WALSH: I could, Phineas, but why should I? Answer me that?

Walsh gets to his feet as he speaks, suddenly catches sight of the glass jar on the counter. He recoils a little and looks at Barnum.

WALSH *continuing:* Do you see the same thing I do?

BARNUM *always the big showman:* Three heads —count 'em!

WALSH *tapping his whiskey bottle with relief:* Thank heaven! The usual triangle, eh?

He picks up the jar, holding it unsteadily. Barnum hovers beside him, ready to catch the jar if Walsh lets it drop. Walsh becomes the true critic.

WALSH: Well, my dear Phineas, this droll mem-

34

ber of the family RANIDAE is a fake.

BARNUM *grabbing for the jar:* Fake? That can't be, Mr. Walsh. Three heads. Impossible.

WALSH: Impossible is the word. There are cases on record where freakish amphibians ...

BARNUM: Who?

WALSH *going on:* Where dizzy-looking frogs are produced by scientists puncturing the eggs. But THREE HEADS! *He grunts:* Even with the aid of THIS ... *Indicating the whiskey bottle:* ... utterly impossible.

BARNUM *awed:* You're powerful smart. *Clutching at a straw:* Couldn't you make a mistake?

WALSH: *I* could, but the frog's papa couldn't. Phineas, freaks are BORN, not MADE.

BARNUM *reflecting:* Mebbe so.

WALSH: Two of those heads are SEWN *on.* See the stitches?

BARNUM *betrayed:* Sewed on! *Through his teeth:* A miscarriage of justice! *With a self-accusing moan:* Mr. Walsh, there's a sucker born every minute.

WALSH: You're not a sucker, P. T. Only a trifle gullible.

BARNUM *dazed:* What'd you say I was, Mr. Walsh?

WALSH *a solemn pronouncement:* A gullibilist is one who wishes to believe everything he WANTS to believe. ...

35

BARNUM *a skyrocket on the rise:* You've hit it. Plumb on the nose. That's what the public is . . . a . . . lot of . . . of . . .

WALSH *prompts him:* Gullibilists.

BARNUM: Ain't it the truth? *Scratches his head:* Do yuh know, I think the 'Merican public acktully likes to be humbugged!

WALSH *airily:* You never uttered a truer word, Phineas.

BARNUM *waxing confidential:* Now look, Mr. Walsh. I got my eye on a empty livery stable in Nassau Street. The very place for a museum. With my ideas and your brains. . . .

WALSH *waves aside the compliment:* My brains? A fake. Everything's a fake. People are the REAL monstrosities, not three-headed frogs or fur-bearing snails. *He grows bitterly vehement:* I'm a fake. You're a fake.

BARNUM *bringing in a minority report:* Don't belittle yourself, Mr. Walsh. . . .

WALSH *lifts his bottle:* Only one thing NOT a fake. . . . *Barnum watches him fondle the almost-empty bottle:* WHISKEY!

Walsh takes a long pull at the flask. As he removes it from his lips, his eyes grow glassy. He staggers. Barnum jumps to the rescue but is late. Walsh careens against the harness rack, which topples, knocking over a show case with a great clatter.

CUT TO:

36

20 INTERIOR: Kitchen – Flash – Barnum's Living Quarters

On SOUND TRACK we hear the commotion from downstairs. Nancy stops, paralyzed, in her tracks.

> NANCY *crying out to Ellen, who appears at the door:* He's MURDERED your uncle! *She starts forward.*

CUT TO:

21 INTERIOR: Barnum's Store

Walsh lies on the floor, and not of this world. Barnum kneels over him, trying to revive the gentleman. The growling of thunder comes from outside, and the rain plays a drum-solo on the window panes.

> BARNUM *to his idol:* Don't die, Mr. Walsh. . . . You and me got a big future. Millions. PLEASE don't die.

Nancy rushes into the scene, terrorized, followed by Ellen. But as soon as she sees which is the victim, she looks on Walsh with contempt. She pauses on the stair landing, but Ellen, with a cry, hastens down. Barnum sees them.

> BARNUM: Help me lift him to the bedroom.

Ellen kneels beside Barnum. She dabs Walsh's head tenderly with her kerchief.

37

NANCY *doubting her ears:* That drunk in OUR bedroom?

BARNUM: He's not drunk. Just somethin' he et. . . .

ELLEN *Florence Nightingale bewildered:* He won't open his eyes, Uncle Phineas. *She rises.*

BARNUM *a captain on the bridge:* Get a doctor.

Ellen starts for the door.

---

22   INTERIOR: Barnum's Store — Shot Through Door

SHOOTING TOWARD street to indicate the storm outside. Ellen is at the door.

NANCY *calling after her:* Ellen! Come back here. It's raining.

Ellen pays no attention but goes out, slamming the door after her. She scurries through the downpour, crossing the street.

DISSOLVE TO:

---

23   INTERIOR: Upper Hall Outside Bedroom Door Barnum's Living Quarters — Night

---

The door to the bedroom is closed. Barnum stands, facing it. He is worried. Ellen stands beside the closed door, greatly concerned and holding a lighted candle. The door opens and the doctor comes out.

DOCTOR *to Barnum:* Acute alcoholism. I've done what I could.

BARNUM: But if he stopped drinkin', Doc....

DOCTOR: Only the tomb stops THIS kind.... *He starts out of scene.*

Barnum is dazed. Nancy comes into scene, arms folded.

NANCY *a woman born to command:* Get him out of here. A charity clinic.

BARNUM *a bruised but desperate gentleman:* Your father used to preach that Charity begins at home.

He starts inside the bedroom, closing the door in Nancy's face.

CUT TO:

---

24   INTERIOR: Barnum's Bedroom—Barnum's Living Quarters

This is a room done in the New England manner, including a feather bed, on which Mr. Walsh is stretched in a stupor. Barnum comes over and looks down at his friend.

BARNUM: You're goin' on the water wagon, Mr. Walsh.

DISSOLVE TO:

This also has the New England aura. There are family portraits—rigidly chaste frames which fence in Plymouth Rock faces, cold with holy repressions. In one corner is an organ, at which Nancy sits, singing. This instrument has an asthmatic, tootling tone, and the singer, who is rendering "Believe Me If All Those Endearing Young Charms," is curdling her theme, murdering this harmonic whimsy with pious aplomb—a small-town choir soprano straining the gizzard with a diet of sharps.

> BARNUM'S VOICE *on* SOUND TRACK, *muffled and petulant:* Nan-cy. . . .

The singer does not hear him. Barnum appears in the doorway, bedraggled and half dressed. He is in stocking feet, and carries his shoes. His hair is mussed, his eyes bleary, his shirt tail hanging out like a balloon jib. He pleads with her; she turns, stopping in the midst of a verse, but the organ playing goes on with a whinnied pianissimo.

> BARNUM: If you GOTTA sing, couldn't you make it softer? I was almost asleep, and . . .

We hear pounding on a door. Nancy stops playing. They both listen.

> WALSH'S VOICE *on* SOUND TRACK: Let me out of here! *He yodels.* Aa-de-lay-e-e-e-hoooo!

Barnum runs, dropping his shoes, stumbling, picking

them up and going out, as Nancy looks after him grimly
and begins to play violently.

CUT TO:

---

26   INTERIOR: Hall Outside Barnum's Door

Barnum drops his shoes to unlock the door quickly.
He opens door, picks up shoes and goes in.

CUT TO:

---

27   INTERIOR: Barnum's Bedroom

Walsh is in delirium, fighting to escape, as Barnum
clinches with him.

> BARNUM *trying to con the patient:* There, there,
> Mr. Walsh. Back to bed . . .

Walsh makes a pass at Mr. Barnum, a glancing blow
to the chin.

> WALSH: Give me a drink or I'll kill you.

Barnum manages to get Walsh across the bed.

> BARNUM *almost winded:* Relax, Mr. Walsh.

> WALSH *struggling out of Barnum's grasp:* I
> want a drink!

Barnum picks up his shoe.

> BARNUM *wielding the shoe:* I hate to do this,
> Mr. Walsh.

He crowns the maniac, knocking him out across the
bed. He now tucks him in tenderly and is worried.

41

BARNUM: Excuse me, Mr. Walsh, but we got a future.

---

28   INTERIOR: Barnum's Living Room

Nancy is standing, sort of eavesdropping at the door, as Ellen appears with a bowl of broth.

NANCY: What's this? Why aren't you in bed?

ELLEN: Some barley broth. He hasn't eaten in three days.

From the bedroom comes the sound of Walsh's voice. He is giving a raving recital in verse. Nancy stands before a portrait of her father, a gentleman with the face of a cliff.

NANCY *to the portrait:* Dear papa! Pray for me.

CUT TO:

---

29   INTERIOR: Barnum's Bedroom

Walsh, in the throes of the jimjams, does his best by a Shakespearian sonnet as he tosses in bed.

WALSH *eloquent with fever:*

"No longer mourn for me when I am dead
Than you shall hear the surly, sullen bell
Give warning to the world that I am fled
From this vile world with vilest worms to
    dwell. . . ."

BARNUM: That's awful morbid, Mr. Walsh. . . .
Walsh opens his eyes and seems to take in Barnum for the first time.

WALSH: Do you know that baby sea-horses, fully formed, are born from their father's chest?

BARNUM *amazed:* Honest? You ain't just seein' things again?

WALSH *a sly rascal, fever or not:* One drink, and I'll tell you all about them.

BARNUM: I can't, Mr. Walsh. . . . Couldn't you tell me where to get a sea-horse without a drink?

WALSH: No. *He resumes his poetic mood:*
"Oh, why should the spirit of mortal be proud? Like a fast flying meteor. . . ."

BARNUM: Shut up! *A showman on the scent:* Excuse me! Now these sea-horses. Can you saddle 'em?

WALSH: I'll tell you this much: They have the body of a stallion and the tail of a fish.

BARNUM: Jumpin' Jehosophat! How big? You can confide in me.

WALSH *calling off all bets:* No, you don't. That's all—until I get my drink.

Barnum is at grips with his conscience. He is on his feet, walking to the door, sorely tempted to yield. Walsh watches him shrewdly. Suddenly Barnum wheels.

BARNUM *Satan loses a decision:* No, sir. Your

brains is worth more to me than a HUNDRED sea-horses.

WALSH *in a fury:* You'll regret this to your dying day.

He tries to get up but falls back weakly, turning his head to the wall. Barnum is about to assist him as there is a knock.

ELLEN'S VOICE *on* SOUND TRACK—*from outside door:* It's me, Uncle Phineas. . . .

Barnum hesitates, looks at the collapsed Walsh, then goes to the door and unlocks it. Ellen comes in with the bowl of broth.

BARNUM: He won't eat a thing.

ELLEN: Let ME try. You go get your supper.

CUT TO:

---

30   CLOSEUP: Walsh

He has heard. He has a cunning look and turns his head on the pillow.

WALSH: Certainly I'll eat . . . if Ellen feeds me.
PULL CAMERA BACK to include Ellen, Barnum and Walsh.

ELLEN *a happy lass:* Would you, Mr. Walsh? *To Barnum:* See?

BARNUM *is dubious:* All right, Ellie. Mr. Walsh is a gentleman. *He exits.*

44

31   CLOSEUP: Ellen

Walsh appraises her as she sits in a chair beside the bed.

> ELLEN *tries to feed him:* I've been praying for you, Mr. Walsh.
>
> WALSH *rises to his elbow, disdaining the soup:* Now listen, child, forget the soup and get me a drink.
>
> ELLEN: Of water?
>
> WALSH: I see. A case of arrested mentality.

32   CLOSEUP: Walsh and Ellen

Ellen looks at him bewildered. Walsh rolls over in bed and turns his back on her, giving up. Then another thought strikes him—another scheme. We see his eyes gleam, and we know that he is up to a trick. He turns back to her with an innocently manufactured smile. Indicating the closed door through which Barnum recently passed, Walsh says:

> WALSH: Would you mind opening the door a trifle, Ellen? The room seems stuffy.

Ellen is only too eager to be of assistance. She quickly opens the door and returns to the chair at the side of the bed. Walsh watches her like a reformed hyena. His scheme is as follows: He intends to grab her in his arms, kiss her, and force her to scream. Barnum and Nancy will hear the yammering, rush into the room, and this will mean Walsh's liberation, as he knows that even Barnum will not tolerate a lecherous scoundrel in the house. The moment Ellen sits down, Walsh starts to put on his act. He manufactures a licentious look, seizes her in his arms and kisses her flush on the mouth. To his great surprise, she doesn't scream. He repeats the kiss. She melts in his embrace, and her arms go around his neck as she returns the kiss. Walsh blinks and looks dazed. He sits up in bed and pushes her away from him.

> WALSH: Why didn't you scream?
>
> ELLEN *calf-eyed:* What for?
>
> WALSH: So your uncle would hear, and throw me on the spears.

Ellen's eyelids droop, and she snuggles closer.

> ELLEN: I couldn't scream, Mr. Walsh. I could cry for joy. I didn't know that you really cared— I thought *I* was the only one that cared.

Walsh's first impulse is to laugh in her face, but her obvious sincerity and innocence hold him in check. He feels a little ashamed of himself. He stutters and stammers, not knowing what to say—not wanting to disillusion her.

> ELLEN *continues:* I'm not afraid to say that I love you, Mr. Walsh. I've always been in love with you—and I don't care what Aunt Nancy says or what anyone says.

46

There are tears in her eyes as she speaks. Walsh would give a million dollars to be somewhere else. Her sincerity has crushed him. When he does not answer, Ellen looks at him searchingly, almost frightened.

ELLEN: You *do* care for me just a little, don't you?

Walsh regains his composure.

WALSH: You're very young, just a child. You've plenty of time to think about love when you're a little older.

Ellen presses his hand between hers, as if afraid she is losing him.

ELLEN: I know I'm young, Mr. Walsh, but I also know age or nothing else is going to make me change. If you'll only wait for me, I promise you'll never be sorry. You will wait, won't you—*please,* Mr. Walsh?

Thus, the burden of the whole situation is placed in the lap of Mr. Walsh. With a magnanimous gesture, he bends over and kisses Ellen's hand.

WALSH: I promise not to fall in love with anyone else until you're of age. . . . How's that?

ELLEN *thrilled beyond words:* I'll count the days —I'll count the hours!

Walsh squirms a trifle, but, after all, there's nothing else for him to do.

ELLEN *picks up the bowl of broth again and, offering it to him, says:* Now, please, Mr. Walsh, won't you take some broth—*just for me?*

47

Walsh hesitates, but the look in her eyes, the pleading in her voice, get him. He starts taking the broth, as the scene

FADES OUT:

FADE IN:

---

33   EXTERIOR: Barnum's Store – Day – Shooting from Exterior Barnum's Store to Door

---

A flint-faced gentleman with a bill-collector's pallor is just entering the store. The *bell jangles* as he goes in and shuts the door. No sooner has he popped in than another gentleman, also callous of puss, comes into the scene from the opposite direction and enters the shop. Again the *bell jangles*. A third man, perhaps a lawyer —he looks hawk-like and as serious as a blood-letter— starts into the emporium. Once again the *bell jangles*. These are brief shots.

CUT TO:

---

34   INTERIOR: Barnum's Store

Nancy is standing in the center of a baiting group of six men, including the three who have just entered. Her arms are folded and she gazes at them defiantly. She is near the stove.

FIRST MAN: Mr. Barnum refuses to give MY firm a serious answer.

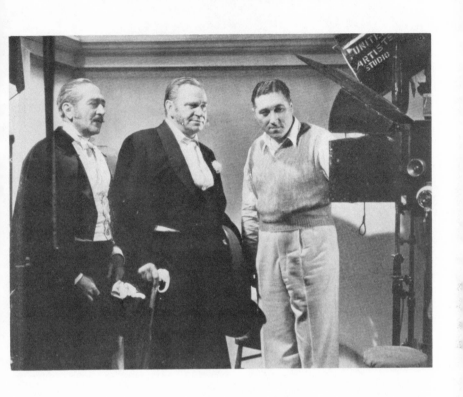

Left to right—Adolphe Menjou, Wallace Beery and Walter Lang, director.

SECOND MAN: He's neglected to pay MY company for seven months. Twenty-six dollars and forty-two cents is the sum involved.

One of the group lets go with a tobacco-stream at the stove. Nancy glares at him.

NANCY: You're not at home.

THIRD MAN *the saliva-shooter:* Beg pardon, madam, but your husband can't put ME off any longer.

NANCY: You'll get your money.

FOURTH MAN: I hope we all live that long. Frankly, Mrs. Barnum, we're forced to resort to the sheriff. A dispossess.

The third man, he of the cuddy, is preparing for another bit of target practice. Nancy restrains him with her eye. He reconsiders, looks around for a spittoon, then holds everything, gesturing his hopelessness.

SECOND MAN: In some ways, mark you, Mr. Barnum's a smart man, but a dreamer. Eccentric.

FIFTH MAN *a gallant bravo:* Our sympathy, of course, is with YOU.

NANCY *clips off the words:* Save your sympathy.

She dabs another glance at the tobacco spitter, who is having difficulty in retaining. She addresses this yeoman.

NANCY *continuing:* Have YOU anything more to say?

The victim gurgles, shrugs, swallows and is terrified.

49

FIRST MAN *to his colleagues:* Gentlemen, we MUST take legal action. *As they nod, he addresses Mrs. Barnum:* The fact is, you are married to a shilly-shally dreamer, a hopeless nincompoop.

NANCY *exploding:* Stop!

FOURTH MAN: He's headed straight for the poorhouse.

SECOND MAN: A man of his loose character ...

Nancy stiffens, lifts her chin and glares.

NANCY: Just leave his character out of this. Who are YOU? A lot of ugly harpies. Phineas T. Barnum's honest and God-fearing. *She turns on the second man:* YOU reek of whiskey. Phineas T. Barnum don't.

NANCY *continuing—to the plug-chawer:* You're smelly with tobacco. Phineas Barnum ain't low and filthy.

During this speech, the CAMERA HAS RUN UP to a—

---

35   CLOSEUP: Nancy

Her eyes are ablaze and she is panting.

NANCY *continuing: To them all in general:* He's got the heart of a child, and you got hearts of stone. One more word and I'll scratch your eyes out. *A bomb-thrower in action:* Now go. All of you. Git!

On SOUND TRACK we hear the jangle of bells six times

in quick succession, indicating the retreat of the collectors. Nancy stands, a triumphant Amazon. She picks up some paper to rub the stain from the stove as CAMERA PULLS BACK to—

---

36   INTERIOR: Barnum's Store—Full Shot

The store is empty, save for Nancy. At this moment the door from the living quarters landing opens cautiously. Mr. Barnum peers out like a clam from its shell. He smiles with an eavesdropper's elation after having heard a good thing of himself. He starts to tiptoe down the steps.

Nancy is courageously humming the air of *"Believe Me If All Those Endearing Young Charms,"* but is sort of wilted in voice and manner.

> BARNUM *the solicitous spouse:* Don't burn yourself, honey. *No answer from his defender, who continues humming. He is tender and grateful:* I heard every word you said, honey. They can't call ME names like that. . . .
>
> NANCY *wheeling from her task, her song ceasing abruptly, her eyes narrowing:* THEY can't, but *I* can.

The great man winces through sheer amazement at this groin-blow.

> NANCY: Every last word they said was true!

His jowls quiver with deflation. He is like a child who

has had a lollipop knocked right out of his mouth by an unexpected slap.

BARNUM *a harpoon in his heart of oak:* You don't MEAN that, Nancy.

NANCY *with a catch in her voice:* Yes, I do. *The tear-ducts begin to function:* Phineas, why can't you be like other men? *The lachrymose display upsets our hero:* Don't you owe SOMETHING to me?

BARNUM *a child resigned to Destiny:* Hmmmm-m-m. Seems I owe everybody. *He amends his remark, backing and filling:* I owe you everything, Nancy. Don't cry.

NANCY *as he pats her shoulder:* We'll be homeless. Nowhere to go. And WHY? *She points to the shelves of glass-imprisoned oddities:* Because your head is full of nasty serpents! Worse'n the one that corrupted poor Adam 'n' Eve.

BARNUM *a showman at any cost:* Oooo! I wish I had THAT snake! *An afterthought:* With proof!

NANCY *letting that one pass:* Worse still, you went and brung a dying drunkard into my bed. A wolf in sheep's clothing. Doctor bills! Medicine by the gallon. . . . *She stops suddenly:* Do you know how much's left in the money till?

BARNUM *woolgathering, he rouses:* Till what?

NANCY *does some pointing:* There's exactly two dollars and eleven cents in that till.

BARNUM: 'Scuse me. I was thinkin'.

52

He is fumbling with a jar of candy, becoming irked when the lid sticks on. He finally wrestles it open. She grunts. He hems a bit, then tries to wheedle.

BARNUM *continuing:* Nancy. . . . *No answer. He tries bribery. He holds a stick of candy to her:* Pep'mint. *She pays no attention, so he starts sucking on it himself:* Reminds me when I was a boy and over-et. *He keeps glancing around at her, hoping she will weaken. She doesn't. He attacks his candy stick rather gloomily:* Guess you're right, Nancy. *She is lost in her mood:* Yep. Connecticut's where we belong, both of us. *She begins to take notice. He adds hastily:* Of course we can't go till we pay our bills. Then also there's the railroad fare, too. It's an awful long walk.

NANCY *has perked up some:* Is that all that's stopping you, Phineas?

BARNUM *lapping at the candy—crunching some sorrowfully—shaking his head:* What else is there to hold me in this citya heartbreaks? What good am I? . . . I took and wasted all our money—fur dreams what turned out to be nightmares. I've made you unhappy. . . . I'm jest a failure, Nancy. I don't belong here. . . . *Sighs:* Ef ever we can get enough money to go back from where we come. . . .

NANCY *more and more thrilled and convinced as she listens—comes close to him, adjusting his coat which is buttoned the wrong way:* P. T., I've got a secret to tell you. . . .

53

BARNUM *puzzled and a trifle afraid:* You don't mean you're ... *He flounders:* ...you're—you've gone and ... You're gonna have a ...

NANCY *flushing at the obstetrical implication:* No. Not that.... *She sighs as though she wishes she were, but Barnum looks relieved. Then she finishes with spirit:* I'd be afraid to. It'd probably have five legs.

BARNUM *intrigued:* Say! THERE'S an idea! Imagine how the crowds ...

NANCY *astounded:* Mr. Barnum! And about your own flesh and blood!

He tries to be coy.

BARNUM: I was only foolin'....

She is hardly convinced.

NANCY: I hope so.... *She brings a bulky letter from wherever ladies carried letters in that golden era:* Phineas Taylor Barnum—we CAN go home to Connecticut.

Barnum appears dazed.

NANCY *continuing:* We can pay our bills, every last penny, and have money for railroad tickets.

He is startled and watches her fearfully as she extracts some bills from the fat envelope—$250, to be exact. He could be no more amazed if she had pulled out rabbits.

BARNUM: Are they real?

NANCY *with dignity:* PAPA sent them.

54

BARNUM *drily:* That ain't answerin' my question.

NANCY: Ain't you ashamed? Two hundred and fifty dollars...

BARNUM *staggered:* A king's ransom.

NANCY *continuing:* Papa sent it on condition we'd pay up and come back to Connecticut for good.

BARNUM: Them Scotchmen get their money's wuth. . . . *Catching her look:* I mean—it was nice of the old man.

NANCY *relenting:* Phineas, can I TRUST you with this cash?

BARNUM *a bit bruised:* Why don't you stick a knife inside me?

NANCY *hands him the money rather gingerly:* I didn't mean anything. I just got to be sure. Now go pay the bills and BRING BACK THE RAILROAD TICKETS!

As Barnum looks at the money incredulously, we hear on SOUND TRACK—

WALSH'S VOICE: Help your old grandpa. . . . We hear Ellen's laugh, and then Ellen and Walsh appear through the door to the landing. Ellen's eyes are glowing. Walsh is dressed for the street. He looks thinner and more subdued, and is, to the surprise of God himself, sober for the first time in many years. Barnum, looking up, is both amazed and pleased. Nancy watches this reappearance of the household ghost with great foreboding.

BARNUM *hastening forward to assist Walsh:*
Mr. Walsh! It's good to see you up. *Amazed:*
Why, you're DRESSED!

WALSH: Civilization demands it of us. Now, in
the African Congo ...

BARNUM *ignoring this:* Your stren'th all right?

WALSH: Another week on my back, and I'll be
ready to be worn out again.

NANCY *pointedly:* Another week! *Raising her
eyebrows:* Phineas. . . .

Barnum looks puzzled, but dutifully answers the sum-
mons and steps aside with Nancy.

C U T   T O :

---

37   CLOSEUP: Nancy and Barnum

Talking in a corner.

NANCY *in a loud voice:* About those last crackers we ordered. . . . *Drops her voice to an undertone:* Get rid of him. Explain we're leavin' town.
He can spend that week on his back somewheres
else. If you don't tell him, I'll—

BARNUM *cutting in:* I'LL tell him. I kin break it
to him gentle and peaceful-like.

ELLEN'S VOICE *on* SOUND TRACK: We're just
going for a little air, Aunt Nancy.

The bell on the door jangles. Nancy whirls around,

56

giving P. T. a meaningful look over her shoulder.

CUT TO:

38   INTERIOR: Barnum's Store – Longer Shot

Ellen and Walsh are at the door, which is half open.
NANCY: Ellen, you stay right here. . . . *With a meaningful look to Barnum to carry out orders immediately:* Your Uncle Phineas kin give him the air.
BARNUM *starting forward like a criminal going to the noose:* Your aunt is right, Ellie. I'LL escort Mr. Walsh.
Ellen is pouting, crushed.
BARNUM *as he joins Walsh at the door—takes his arm:* I hope your stren'th holds up, Mr. Walsh.
They start out the door.
NANCY *pointedly, to Barnum:* See that YOURS does too, Phineas Barnum.
Barnum gives her a hang-dog, reproachful look, as the two men exit through the door, closing it with the aftermath of jangling bells.

DISSOLVE TO:

39   EXTERIOR: Street – Follow Shot of Barnum and Walsh – Day

Barnum is handling Walsh with the delicacy of an escort squiring the fragile Camille. Barnum is talking.

57

BARNUM *sadly:* . . . And Mr. Walsh, this is the darkest hour of my life, but I gotta do it. . . . I gotta ast you to leave. *Walsh makes an amused, deprecatory gesture:* One more month, and I coulda finished your cure. . . . *Waxing enthusiastic:* . . . brung back fur prosterity them magnificent brain cells o' yourn. *Walsh is amused, but Barnum wags his head mournfully:* Instead, what happens? I'm a failure—I gotta go back to Connecticut. . . .

WALSH *with a whimsical smile:* A disciple with an unsaved soul—a thwarted genius. The world's foremost entrepreneur of freaks reduced to milking cows.

Barnum takes the word "entrepreneur" big, but before he can comment, Walsh glances at the sign of a grog shop they are passing—"JOE'S SALOON."
The CAMERA STOPS.

WALSH *with enthusiasm:* Let's go in, Phineas.
Barnum's face collapses. All his good work gone by the board.

BARNUM: Should we ought?

WALSH *a convalescing owl:* We should ought.
Walsh passes in first, with Barnum trailing, his soul gnawed by misgivings.

CUT TO:

58

It is a small and tawdry establishment de suds. Walsh bellies up to the bar. The Bar-keep, a gentleman with cow-lick hair and handle-bar moustaches, knows him of old. Other gentlemen are wetting their whistles at this font.

BAR-KEEP: 'Lo, Brother Walsh. . . . where you been hidin'?

WALSH: In jail, Joe. The Bastille. *Barnum is looking sorrowfully at a water-color nude above the bar-mirror:* Meet the Warden, Mr. Barnum.

The bar-keeper genuflects and Barnum nods. Walsh addresses Barnum.

WALSH: What'll it be?

BARNUM *girding his loins with righteousness:* Buttermilk.

The bartender "takes it," smiles—then to Walsh.

BAR-KEEP: Same as USUAL, Mr. Walsh?

He reaches, without waiting, toward a bottle of whiskey. Barnum's heart is in his shoes.

WALSH *full of surprises:* The same as Mr. Barnum, Joe. BUTTERMILK!

Joe is on the verge of apoplexy. Barnum's face lights up. . . . The Bar-keep begins filling two glasses with curdled cow-sap.

BARNUM *mumbling heavenward:* A lost sheep is found. *To Walsh—whacking him on the back:*

59

Congratulations, sir! Congratulations!

Turning to the assembled quaffers, he smashes his fist upon the bar to attract attention.

BARNUM *continuing:* Step right up here—offer your congratulations to this genius plucked from the burnin'...

WALSH *staring whimsically at the glass of buttermilk:* Need we make it quite so public, Phineas?

BARNUM *enthusiasm waxing—leaps on top of a beer keg:* I want the whole world to know it.... *Pointing to Walsh at the bar:* Sirs, you see before you a man who has struggled with the Demon Rum, and triumphed! Wrestled with Satan on the mountain top....

CROWD *ad libbing—rowdy—amused:* That's it, Reverend.... A soul-saver.... Hurrah for the Demon Rum! ... *Others take up the chant:* Three cheers for the Demon Rum!

BARNUM *carried away by enthusiasm:* That's it —three cheers for the Demon Rum! ... *A laugh —he corrects himself:* ... the DOWNFALL of the Demon Rum! Mr. Walsh here, has seed the light. HIS THREE MILLION PRECIOUS BRAIN CELLS IS RESCUED FROM OBLIVIUM.

BARNUM *continuing:* I feel like yellin' out "Hallelujah"! ... *He bellows this out, but amends:* ... but I won't. *He looks at Walsh who has not as yet touched the buttermilk except in suspicious sips:* Just try it, Mr. Walsh.... You'll be surprised.

WALSH *drily:* So will my stomach.

He starts to down the buttermilk.

DISSOLVE TO:

---

41   INTERIOR: Barnum's Living Room

A large trunk is opened, and Nancy is packing heavy woolen coats and underwear. There are carpetbags in the offing.

NANCY *calling out:* Some more moth balls, Ellen.

Ellen comes in slowly, her feet dragging. She is carrying a paper bag of moth balls. Nancy snatches them from her. She is jubilant.

NANCY: What's wrong with you, child? Ain't you happy 'bout goin' back to Connecticut?

ELLEN *her dutiful words give the lie to her look:* Yes. Aunt Nancy....

She exits from the room as heavy footsteps sound on the stairs.

NANCY *calling out:* That you, Phin-ee-as?

BARNUM *speaking before and after he enters:* Uh-huh....

Mr. Barnum seems down-at-the-mouth, an emotion which might be construed as disappointment at being required to leave New York—or a screen for guilt. He yawns.

BARNUM: Whatcha doin'?

He starts to sit down on a rather aged but dressy coat draped on a chair. Nancy halts him.

NANCY: Look out, Phineas! *She picks up the coat:* I'm savin' this to bury you in.

BARNUM *he blinks at the garment:* Can you imagine? I'd plumb forgot that coat.

She is at work on the packing, as he advances to slip an arm about her.

NANCY *affects to throw off the embrace but likes it:* You were married in it. Now don't interrupt the packin'.

BARNUM *a Romeo with a stuttering conscience:* Yes, indeedy. Why, I COURTED you with that there garment. Wasn't the smell of them apple trees tremenjus? And us walkin', a coupla lovebirds, through your father's meadow. *He goes overboard with reminiscence:* The day he caught us kissin' in a haystack?

NANCY: Go 'long, Phineas. . . .

BARNUM: That very night he ast me WHAT was my intentions. Suspicious as a tomcat on a tin roof.

NANCY *reprovingly:* Papa regards you as the son he never had.

BARNUM: You mean like he's never GONNA have.

NANCY *intuition on the job:* Mr. Barnum, did you get the tickets?

BARNUM *in a trap:* Fact of the matter is . . .

62

Nancy forgets the apple blossoms and the meadow.

NANCY: WHERE ARE THOSE TICKETS?

BARNUM *as innocent as a highwayman:* You mean the railroad tickets? Oh, yes ... *A desperate try at being casual:* Well, not exactly ... you see ...

NANCY *the safety valve about to give:* You didn't get them.

BARNUM: Just hold your hosses, Nancy. It kinda mixes me up when a person swarms all over me.... It's tremenjus ... millions in it.... As Mr. Walsh says, colossal!

NANCY: I knew HE figured in it somehow. *Through her teeth:* WHERE IS THAT MONEY?

BARNUM: Quit rushin' me, will yah? Jumpin' Jehosophat, you'd think I was a common, ordinary thief.

NANCY: Mr. WALSH borrow the money?

BARNUM *horrified:* Nancy, if you knew what has happened today, you wouldn't talk that a way. ... A miracle has happened—Mr. Walsh's three million precious brain cells, as well as his soul, has been saved. Me and him is pardners. Remember that barn I allus wanted for a museum?

NANCY: I remember every banana peel you ever slipped on.

BARNUM: You'll have carriages and hosses. I paid down two hundred on the livery stable.

NANCY: And the other fifty? Did you light Mr.

Walsh's cigar with that?

BARNUM: What's the use? *Getting his second wind:* I got it right here. *He pats his breast pocket.*

NANCY: Hand it over.

BARNUM: It ain't goin' to blow up the chimley. ...Yuh don't truss me.

NANCY: I've trusted you too long. That fifty dollars'll take Ellen and me back to Connecticut.

BARNUM *is aghast:* Why, Nancy! You don't mean it....You COULDN'T leave ME.

A child afraid of the dark, he tries to take her in his arms. She pulls away.

NANCY: Give me that money! *As Barnum looks pained:* I've stood all I can, Phineas Barnum!

She starts to crowd him, as he retreats.

BARNUM *retreating—imploringly:* Now, Nancy....

NANCY *advancing on him relentlessly as he backs around the room: Don't* "NANCY" me! It's every penny we got left! Give me that money! THIS INSTANT—or I'll...*At this juncture, poor Barnum backs against a chair and goes over backward. He is on his spine, as Nancy reaches down triumphantly to take the money from his hand:* Now I got it!

From below stairs, we hear the jangling of the door bell. A just God has sent reinforcements to Saint Barnum. The great man scrambles to his feet, still in pos-

64

session of the fifty dollars.

BARNUM *eagerly:* You're all tuckered out, Nancy.... I'll go.

He streaks through the door.

CUT TO:

---

42   INTERIOR: Barnum's Store—Close Shot at Stairway

Showing door of living quarters and a portion of the stairway.

Barnum bolts through the door as though horny Satan were after him. He leans against the jamb a moment, blotting his face with a large bandana. His relief is very evident. Again the bell jangles. Barnum leaps off into space, and down the stairs.

CUT TO:

---

43   INTERIOR: Barnum's Store—Shooting at Back of Store

As Barnum comes careening down the stairs, risking his bones in the panic to get away, we

CUT TO:

---

44   INTERIOR: Barnum's Store—Another Angle

A husky citizen with the face of a fat ferret, Mr. J. P. SKIFF, half salesman, half blackmailer, is bowing and babbling as Mr. Barnum comes within range.

SKIFF: Mr. Barnum? Skiff's the name. J. P. Skiff. You've probably heard of me in the public prints.

BARNUM: You got the best of me, Mister.

SKIFF: Mr. Barnum, I'm a man of few words. A promoter. *I* gather ideas. You gather freaks.

BARNUM *perks up as the magic word is spoken:* Whacha got, Mister?

SKIFF: Skiff's the name. *He buttonholes Barnum.* Now s'pose I could deliver the REAL AND GENUWINE nurse of the First President of these glorious United States?

BARNUM *looking toward upstairs:* Not so loud. *He points upstairs.* Sickness. Now let me get this straight. The genuwine nurse of who?

SKIFF: GEORGE WASHINGTON?

BARNUM: Jumpin' Jehosophat!

SKIFF: Josie Heath. One hundred and sixty years of age.

BARNUM *reverently:* Bless her old heart.

SKIFF: I can deliver her lock, stock and barrel. From her own lips she'll tell you how she dangled little George on her knee. She was present the day the prankish little chap cut down the internationally famous cherry tree. She peeled potatoes at Valley Forge when....

The two men have moved toward the door, Skiff sort of luring Barnum on. He is unable to stand it further

66

and interrupts hoarsely.

BARNUM: Where is she? Let me see her!

SKIFF: See her you SHALL! *He opens the door with a grandiloquent gesture and announces:* Josie! Josie Heath!

CUT TO:

---

45   INTERIOR: Barnum's Living Room

Nancy is sitting on the closed trunk. She is disconsolate but determined. Barnum's clothes are scattered about. She is holding the wedding coat. Ellen stands beside her.

ELLEN: Uncle Phineas'd be lost without you.

Nancy drops the coat and picks up her bonnet. She puts it on and begins to tie the strings.

NANCY: Stay here till I get a drayman.

Ellen looks at her protestingly, but Nancy marches out of the room. Ellen starts to pick up Barnum's clothes.

CUT TO:

---

46   INTERIOR: Barnum's Store – Shooting Toward Stairs at Back of Store

---

Nancy, her eyes steeled, marches firmly downstairs. Suddenly she sees something in the store below that attracts her attention. She stops dead on the landing, staring down.

CUT TO:

47   INTERIOR: Barnum's Store — From Nancy's Angle

Skiff is just leaving and Barnum is closing the door on him. But what has magnetized Nancy's eye is a fat Negro woman, who sits on a chair, her feet up on the stove rail, calmly smoking a pipe.

CUT TO:

48   INTERIOR: Barnum's Store — Another Angle to Include All Three

Nancy, recovering from her first jolt, gasps as Barnum looks up at her.

BARNUM *a boy at heart:* Nancy, come here! A bonanza!

Nancy, against her will, moves like an automaton down the steps. Barnum is too excited to notice her mood. He is again the great showman.

BARNUM *continuing:* As Mr. Walsh says, Eureka! *As though addressing an audience:* Step right up, ladies and gentlemen ... Josie Heath! One hundred and ninety-six years old. The real and genuwine nurse of George Washington, the

68

proud Father of his Country.

Nancy stands in a daze and Barnum finishes with a flourish:

BARNUM *continuing:* ... And just think, Nancy, she only cost me fifty dollars!

NANCY: Fifty dollars?

The dam bursts. It's too much. She starts to faint, and Barnum catches her, easing her to the floor where she lies supine.

BARNUM *to Josie:* You're a nurse—what should I oughtta do?

JOSIE *not interested—spits upon the stove:* Git her a sluga gin—and git me one, too, while you're at it!

Barnum, who has been working over Nancy, straghtens up, completely forgetting his unconscious spouse.

BARNUM *horrified:* What would the Father of our Country say if he heard you talk like that!

FADE OUT:

FADE IN:

---

49   INTERIOR: Barnum's Museum—Close Shot at Platform on Which Josie Heath is exhibited—Day

---

(This Museum is the first—the converted livery stable. It is a one-story affair, although we might take the license of using it as the nucleus for the great American

Museum he later acquires.)

Josie Heath is seated on the platform, with signs all about her proclaiming her as Washington's nurse. There is a large picture of Washington, American flags, a cherry tree chopped in half, with the hatchet still in the tree, adorning one side of the platform.

Barnum stands on the platform with Josie, exhibiting her and pointing to her with a long stick.

> BARNUM *speaking as scene opens:* And now, Ladies and Gentlemen, if you'll kindly step up around the platform, I'll have the honor of presenting Josie Heath. . . .

CUT TO:

---

50 INTERIOR: Barnum's Museum – Longer Shot

Showing the long platform divided into booths. Here are the tattooed man, the rubber woman, etc., strange animals—a cow with two heads. We see wax works depicting the coronation of Queen Victoria, an axe murderer at work, and other whimsical tableaux. The place is jammed to capacity.

> BARNUM'S VOICE *continuing — over* SOUND TRACK: . . . The oldest living woman in the world. Josie Heath is one hundred and ninety-nine years old. . . .

CUT TO:

51   CLOSE SHOT AT PLATFORM — INTERIOR: Barnum's Museum

Barnum is continuing his spiel, as the crowd gapes at Josie curiously.

>BARNUM *continuing:* One more year, come April, and she'll of lived two whole centuries. Am I right, Josie?
>
>JOSIE *without much enthusiasm—sucking at her pipe:* Whatevah you all says goes, Massa Barnum.

There is a laugh from the audience. Barnum covers up his discomfiture by patting the wench's back.

>BARNUM *to the crowd:* Gentlemen, THERE's a wife for you. She's been trained right. *A sally of laughter.* Now pass right along, and see the rest of these tremenjus exhibits—freaks that has mystified crowned heads and other scientists.

CUT TO:

52   INTERIOR: Barnum's Museum — Medium Shot at Ticket Offices

There are three ticket offices near the entrance, and in them three girls selling tickets as fast as they can make change. Ellen is one of the box-office girls.
Walsh is standing before Ellen's booth, talking to an attendant whom we shall call Tod. During the ensuing

scene, Barnum's voice can be heard faintly in the background still spieling.

> BARNUM'S VOICE *faintly—on* SOUND TRACK:
> Don't forget the two-headed cow, a sacred beast stolen by pirates from the Sultan of Borneo ...
>
> C U T   T O :

---

53   INTERIOR: Barnum's Museum – Close Shot at Ellen's Ticket Office

---

Showing Ellen selling tickets to the public.   During the six months which have passed, Ellen has burgeoned into young womanhood. Walsh, considerably changed, elegantly sober, is near Ellen's booth talking with the attendant. He is handing Tod a long, impressive envelope. As Ellen passes out tickets and makes change, she casts surreptitious, adoring glances in Walsh's direction.

> WALSH *tersely—to Tod:* ... And take this full-page ad to the *Globe.* Tell Mr. Greeley we expect, in return, three one-column stories, with particular reference to the thousands turned away daily....
> *As Tod starts out.* And tell him not to slip up on that man-eating rabbit story. *Turns abruptly to Ellen as Tod exits:* Pardon me, Ellen—what were you saying?
> ELLEN *covered with confusion:* Nothing, Mr. Walsh—only ... *she pauses to give change to a*

customer . . . every day I look at you—you seem to grow—*she gulps* . . . handsomer and handsomer. . . .

Walsh is startled, slightly amused.

WALSH *whimsically:* I can't deceive you, Ellen. . . . *Pulls up his sleeves, getting over he has nothing concealed up them:* . . . It's merely the new hair tonic I'm using. . . .

At this moment, Barnum bursts into the scene. He is perspiring and puffing like a walrus.

BARNUM *to Ellen:* Stop sellin' tickets—much as it breaks my heart. The place is jammed—we can't get 'em out. Three women fainted. . . . *Gives a weary "Phew."* They left the biggest one fur me to carry out.

WALSH *smiles:* We can't make the "Exit" sign any larger, P. T. It covers the entire wall now.

BARNUM *nods dismally—then scratches his head:* Ain't there no other word for Exit?

WALSH: Um-mm. . . . Yes—"Egress," for example. *Spells it.* E-g-r-e-s-s.

Barnum's face lights up with the birth of an idea.

BARNUM: That gives me a idee. What'd I do without your brains, Mr. Walsh? *Whirls around—calls off:* Hey, Sam. . . .

He rushes out of scene. Walsh looks after him, amused.

CUT TO:

73

54 INTERIOR: Barnum's Museum – Another Angle

Sam, a workman dressed in overalls, is carrying a large bucket of whitewash as Barnum bursts in. He pauses. Before Barnum can speak to Sam, however, the "Josie Heath selling" Skiff appears in the background.

SKIFF *calling:* Mr. Barnum. . . .

BARNUM *turns, sees Skiff—very effusively:* Sir, to you. . . . *Extends his hand as Skiff comes up.* The right hand of fellowship, Mr. Skiff.

SKIFF *meaningfully:* I'd like to talk to you in private. . . .

BARNUM: Sure thing. Join you in my office.

Skiff starts toward the office. Barnum turns to the workman, Sam, starts to talk to him, and in pantomime, indicates a large sign.

CUT TO:

55 INTERIOR: Barnum's Outer Office – Medium Shot

Skiff comes into the office. Nancy has just spread out Barnum's lunch, which she has brought in a pail. She is pouring a glass of milk as Skiff enters and does not look up.

SKIFF *a breath of optimism:* Good morning.

74

Nancy glances up, gives him a curt nod. She is not the one to conceal her dislikes. Undaunted, Skiff expands.

SKIFF *continuing:* Lucky Barnum. . . . *Glances at the food.* Now if I could only find a wife who'd appreciate ME, as you—

NANCY *curtly interrupting:* Jest wastin' your time looking.

Skiff, taken aback somewhat, goes blank. Barnum enters very effusively, and places his hand on Skiff's shoulder.

BARNUM: Have you brung me another bonanza?

NANCY *to Barnum:* Eat this while it's hot, Phineas.

BARNUM *to Nancy:* Business first, Nancy. *He quails under her stern look—waves Skiff into his private office.* Be with you in a minute, Mr. Skiff.

Skiff exits into Barnum's private office, bowing to Nancy, who looks straight through him.

BARNUM *beaming after Skiff:* Sweet character!

NANCY *looking after Skiff:* Looks like a sneak thief.

BARNUM *shushing her lest Skiff hear:* You don't know human nature when you see it.

At this moment, Walsh comes dashing in. He has a letter in his hand and is in a dither.

WALSH: She's ours, Phineas. . . . Signed on the dotted line for two thousand dollars.

NANCY *gasping:* Two thousand dollars!

BARNUM *to Nancy:* And cheap at half the price.

75

... The greatest freak of the century—Madame Zorro, the one and only Bearded Lady! *To Walsh:* When does she get here?

WALSH *consulting letter:* Soon as she finishes her contracts in Italy.

NANCY *grimly:* Phineas Barnum, do I understand you to say that you're bringin' over a lady with a beard?

BARNUM *indicating knee-length muff:* Two fathoms of spinach.

NANCY: You're temptin' Providence, Phineas. She CAN'T be a lady.

C U T   T O :

---

56   INTERIOR: Barnum's Private Office – Barnum's Museum

Skiff is standing close to the door leading to the outer office, his ear glued to the portal, listening. BARNUM'S VOICE *on* SOUND TRACK—*coming from other side of door:* But she IS a lady!

C U T   T O :

---

57   INTERIOR: Barnum's Outer Office – Barnum's Museum

Nancy looks at Barnum suspiciously.
    NANCY: How do you know?

76

BARNUM: All them Yurrup-peons who's seed her, says she's a lady.

NANCY *the District Attorney:* How do THEY know?

BARNUM *baffled for the moment—then triumphantly:* Nancy, you can't fool a foreigner about THEM matters.

Before Nancy can react to this, Barnum disappears into the inner office. Walsh has a sudden fit of coughing, and is obliged to hide his face behind a handkerchief.

CUT TO:

---

58   INTERIOR: Barnum's Private Office—Barnum's Museum

Skiff barely has time to duck from his keyhole position to the center of the room as Barnum comes in. He closes the door behind him, carefully locking it.

BARNUM: Sorry to keep you waitin', Mr. Skiff. *He brightens.* Got some good news for me?

SKIFF: The exact opposite. It concerns yon Josie Heath.

BARNUM: Smallpox?

SKIFF: We've made a terrible mistake, me and you. . . .

BARNUM *is dazed:* She ain't married?

SKIFF: Worse, Mr. Barnum. Josie Heath's a

FAKE. She AIN'T one hundred and sixty years old. . . .

BARNUM *unconsciously correcting him:* A hundred 'n' NINETY-NINE.

SKIFF: She's only eighty. And what's more, she never even HEARD of George Washington—except in your speeches. Don't interrupt. This smoky wench is a runaway slave from Georgia.

Groggy, Barnum sits down, his jowls in his hands. Skiff continues.

SKIFF *continuing:* And her owner, Colonel Snodgrass, is after her.

BARNUM: This IS a shock, Skiff. A blow to my vanity. Why, she's my best drawin' card. *His mood changes.* But am I mad? No, sir. It's worth it all, Skiff. . . .

BARNUM *continuing—he gets to his feet, extends his hand, and Skiff takes it warily, not knowing why:* . . . to meet an honest man. Congratulations for coming smack up here with the truth, to keep me from humbuggin' an innocent public. Congratulations. Now gimme back the fifty dollars I paid you.

SKIFF: Oh, no, Mr. Barnum. I pay you nothin'. YOU PAY me—one thousand—now. In cash.

BARNUM *at sea without a rudder:* You confuse me, sir.

SKIFF: It'll cost you exactly one thousand dollars to keep my mouth shut. Or should I expose

78

you in Mr. Greeley's newspaper, the *Globe?*
BARNUM *his soul torn:* Lemme get this straight.
SKIFF: You got it straight. Come across.
BARNUM *slow rage mounting:* Jumpin' Jehoso-
phat! *Advances upon Skiff.* You—you BLACK-
MAILER!

He lets go with a roundhouse swing to the jaw. Skiff
wobbles, but comes back. Barnum is infuriated now—
a Berserker with a mission. They mill about the room,
bowling over furniture. First one is down, and then
the other.

CUT TO:

---

59   INTERIOR:

As Nancy and Walsh hear the four-ply rumpus
from the inner office, Nancy lets out a terrified yip.
Walsh rushes to the door, trying to open it, but it is
locked. Walsh pounds on it.
WALSH: Phineas!
There is a Gargantuan crash from the next room.
Nancy's hands are clasped in prayer as the building
shakes to its foundation.

CUT TO:

---

60   INTERIOR: Barnum's Private Office

The fight is still on, both men rolling on the floor. Suddenly Skiff gets free, leaps to the desk, picks up a large

bronze statuette with the intention of crowning Barnum with it, but Barnum, with a bellow, lunges at him. Skiff still has the statuette upraised, but Barnum ignores this, grabs Skiff around the throat, and with his massive dukes lifts him off the floor, shaking him as he would a rat. The *objet d'art* falls from Skiff's grasp. He becomes limp as Barnum chokes him.

> NANCY'S AND WALSH'S VOICES *from outside on* SOUND TRACK: Phin-ee-as! Open that door!

The voices bring Barnum partly back to civilization. He looks at the wilted figure in his grip. Still in a fury, he drags Skiff to the door, unlocks it.

C U T   T O :

---

61   INTERIOR: Barnum's Outer Office

Walsh and Nancy start back aghast, as Barnum, still in a bone-breaking rage, steps out with Skiff, who is beginning to struggle back to life. He picks Skiff up and hurls him out through the door. Skiff lands in a heap in the doorway leading to stairway. Walsh looks at Phineas, purses his lips. He is half-amused, half-amazed at this bull-like display. Nancy is too startled to speak. Skiff lumbers to his feet, shakes his fist at Barnum.

> SKIFF *to Barnum:* You'll regret this to your dying day, you big baboon!

80

Barnum (Wallace Beery) is amazed to hear that Mr. Walsh (Adolphe Menjou) recites Shakespeare while under the influence of strong drink.

BARNUM *takes a step toward him—bellows:* GIT
OUT!

C U T T O :

---

62 INTERIOR: Barnum's Museum—Angle Near
Outside of Barnum's Offices

There is an iron stairway of nine or ten steps giving
from the main part of the Museum to Barnum's offices,
which are on the mezzanine floor. Just outside the
entrance to the office is a small iron platform, and the
stairs lead directly down from this.
Skiff bounds out of the doorway like a scalded cat,
misses his footing on the stairway and does a fall all
the way down. Barnum appears on the landing as Skiff
starts his dive.

BARNUM *shaking his fist after Skiff:* And STAY
out!
Skiff picks himself up from the bottom of the stairs
and starts to run. Barnum turns back into his office,
when something in the Museum below catches his eye.
He stares, surprised. Then a slow grin appears on his
face. He calls over his shoulder into the office.

BARNUM *calling:* Mr. Walsh . . . come here!
Quick! The rainbow after the storm.
Walsh joins him on the platform, and they both look
off. There is a grin on both their faces, as they see. . . .

8 1

63   INTERIOR: Barnum's Museum – Long Shot
      (From Their Angle)

Showing a large sign reading: "THIS WAY TO THE
EGRESS." A large crowd is milling at the door below
the sign, struggling to get through.

CUT TO:

64   INTERIOR: Barnum's Museum – Closer Shot
      of Crowd

Fighting and scrambling under the sign to get through
the door.
      CROWD *ad libbing:* What is an Egress? ... Don't
      push. ... I want to see the Egress. ... Let me
      through. ...

CUT TO:

65   EXTERIOR: Barnum's Museum – Close Shot at
      Other Side of "Egress" Door

Showing crazed people, fighting their way out of the
building.
      CROWD *ad libbing—as they come through door:*
      Where is this Egress? ... What do you suppose it
      is? ...
PULL CAMERA BACK to show—

66 EXTERIOR: Alleyway – Close Shot at Exit Door

As the crowd comes out into the alleyway, through the door, they look about dazed, realizing they are outside. Some laugh, some are furious and try to go back.

CROWD *ad lib:* What's the idea! ... It's a fake!! ... We're outside! ...

FADE OUT:

FADE IN:

67 NEWSPAPER INSERT:

It reads:

"BARNUM EXPOSED AS FAKE
IN JOSIE HEATH SCANDAL"
*Showman Makes Public Apology; Bogus
Nurse of Washington Only
Eighty Years Old*

"Phineas T. Barnum yesterday made a public apology, following close on the heels of the sensational disclosure that Josie Heath not only never saw George Washington, but is merely eighty years old, instead of one hundred and ninety-nine years of age, as hitherto claimed by Barnum. Furthermore, Josie Heath is a runaway slave, the property of Colonel Martin Snodgrass, Kentucky planter. The Colonel took charge of his property yesterday, and almost came to blows with the blustering Barnum. . . ."

DISSOLVE TO:

---

68   ANOTHER NEWSPAPER INSERT:

Which reads:

"GREELEY ACCUSES BARNUM OF ANOTHER HOAX IN EXHIBITING BEARDED LADY TO THE PUBLIC"

"Editor James Gordon Greeley yesterday warned curiosity seekers to think twice before paying their hard-earned money to see P. T. Barnum's latest wonder. The owner of the *Globe* charges editorially that Madame Zorro, the supposed Bearded Lady, is an impostor. Editor Greeley recalled the recent exposure of Josie Heath, and Barnum's false claims that she was one hundred and ninety-nine years old, and had been the nurse of little George Washington. Mr. Greeley adds that Madame Zorro's act is a bald-faced trick of the showman's to lure money from the pockets of patrons."

Through this insert, DOUBLE EXPOSE series of FLASH SCENES—

69   FLASH: Close Shot at Cheap Bar—INTERIOR:
      Saloon

Showing two teamsters arguing, over mugs of beer.
      FIRST TEAMSTER: Liar, am I? *He douses con-
      tents of his beer mug into the other's face.* She's
      a man, I tell you!
      SECOND TEAMSTER *picking up whip standing
      beside him at bar:* Yuh bloomin' mule skinner!
      Cuts his friend across the shoulders with whip.
      It's a woman!
They leap at each other, as we
                              QUICK DISSOLVE TO:

70   FLASH: Close Shot at Dinner Table in
      Middle-Class Home

Around the table sit the father, mother and two kids.
The husband and wife are arguing, as we pick up scene.
      WIFE *indignantly:* You're a fool, Wilbur!
      HUSBAND *indignantly—slamming down his cof-
      fee cup and spilling contents:* I tell yuh, she IS a
      woman!
                              QUICK DISSOLVE TO:

71   FLASH: Close Shot of Two Boys in Alleyway

Fighting. As the scene opens, one boy falls on his back and the other boy jumps on him, gouging at his eyes.

     VICTORIOUS BOY: Say it! Go on, say it! Say it's a man!

QUICK DISSOLVE TO:

72   FLASH – INTERIOR: Barber Shop – Close Shot at Chair

A barber is shaving a customer.

     BARBER *smothering customer's face with lather:* My personal opinion is, she CAN'T be a woman. CUSTOMER *sitting up abruptly, gets the lather brush in his mouth:* Fat-headed fool! She IS a woman!

He sputters and chokes on the lather.

QUICK DISSOLVE TO:

73   FLASH – INTERIOR: Opera House – Close Shot at Box

Containing three of the social élite—two women and a man. On SOUND TRACK, is heard a selection of opera —"NORMA" or "RIGOLETTO."

     WOMAN *grabs husband's arm—in fierce under-*

86

tone: Keep still!

HUSBAND: You started it, saying she's a man!

SECOND WOMAN: Well, she is!

HUSBAND *leaping to his feet:* She's a woman!
He strides out of the box.

The NEWSPAPER INSERT and FLASH SCENES DISSOLVE
OUT, and on the screen we

DISSOLVE TO:

---

74   QUICK MONTAGE CLOSEUPS: Various Heads

Of people of all classes: dowager, servant girl, Negro,
banker, etc.

VOICES OF PEOPLE *as each one speaks:* She's
a woman! ... She bane man! ... Shuah IS a
woman! ... Ridiculous—a MAN! I tell you she's a
woman! She's a man!

DISSOLVE TO:

---

75   INTERIOR: Barnum's Museum – Day – Close
Shot at Platform

On which sits the Bearded Lady in all her glory, as
a gaping crowd surrounds her. She is selling postcards
by the dozens.

CUT TO:

INTERIOR: Barnum's Museum – Longer Shot

Showing people massed around the Bearded Lady's platform, staring at her.

CROWD *ad libbing:* Anyone can see it's a man! ... Certainly, she's a woman.... I'll never read the *Globe* again.... Greeley's a fool! ... Greeley knows what he's talking about....She IS a woman! ... It's a man! ...

CUT TO:

77 INTERIOR: Barnum's Private Office in Museum – Medium Shot of Walsh and Barnum – Night

Walsh is seated at a desk, concocting more copy for the press. Barnum is pacing back and forth, wiping his brow. He is plainly worried.

WALSH *his labors interrupted by the pacing showman:* Phineas, would you mind taking your horse to the park?

BARNUM *his brow furrowed—he makes sad noises:* Ah, ho, hum-mm-m! Ho-ho, hum-mm-m. Dum-m de-die-do....Hah!

WALSH: Stop brooding. If it's Greeley and his editorials, forget it. Think of the publicity he's giving us.

BARNUM *a hollow soothsayer:* Last night, I had a disruptin' vision . . .

WALSH *interrupting:* I warned you against that fourth helping of pig-knuckles.

BARNUM *re-living his adventure in the dream world:* This vision was you and me behind cold prison bars. . . .

WALSH: In the same cell?

BARNUM: This ain't no jokin' matter, Mr. Walsh, and I been thinkin'. Ain't it kinda suspicious, Madame Zorro losin' her birth certificate?

WALSH: On the contrary. Only a WOMAN would lose her birth certificate.

BARNUM: If they was only some way I could be certain. . . .

WALSH: Well, Phineas, after all—you're the owner. . . .

As Barnum gets the drift of this, he flushes like a débutante losing her drawers during a mazurka, looks terror-ridden.

BARNUM *stricken:* But Mr. Walsh, *I* couldn't— I jest COULDN'T!

Walsh shrugs, returns to his scrivening.

WALSH *carelessly:* Very well. I'll send this article to the *Globe*. Greeley's challenged us to prove she's a woman. . . . We accept his challenge.

BARNUM *desperately:* Better hold that up fur a few minutes, Mr. Walsh. . . . *Grabs his hat, and*

89

with a do-or-die air, starts toward the door: This is an emergency!

He exits.

CUT TO:

---

78   INTERIOR: Bearded Lady's Dressing Room

The Bearded Lady is sitting on a chair, curling her beard with a hot iron from a charcoal burner. There is a knock at the door.

ZORRO *in a deep voice:* Come in.

Barnum enters. The bearded one merely nods and offers Barnum a chair, pointing with the iron. He smiles but is a bit uneasy. He does not take the chair but sidles up to the dressing table.

BARNUM: Just dropped in to see if you was comfortable. *His eyes light on some embroidery work which lies on the table. He beams.* That's awful pretty. Course a man don't know 'bout such things.

ZORRO: I got first prize for embroidery in the convent.

BARNUM *relieved, he sits down beside her:* Do your children sew?

ZORRO: Hardly.

BARNUM: You have some dear children, ain't you?

ZORRO *laughs in the bass register:* How could I?

His heart is lead. I'm not married.

BARNUM *again hopeful:* I'm glad to hear THAT.

ZORRO *understanding his coy words:* Does it make THAT much difference to you, Mr. Barnum?

BARNUM *a bit fuddled but game:* Well—you know—the fact is, Madame Zorro. . . . *He gets awkwardly to his feet.*

ZORRO: Must we be so formal—Phineas? Lily's MY name. *She rises—takes a box of cigars from the makeup shelf and offers them:* Smoke?

BARNUM: Never use the weed.

ZORRO *selecting a large one, bites off the end, spits it out and picks up a coal with the curling iron and lights the stogie:* It's better than chewing tobacco. *Puffing:* I had to give THAT up when I had the mumps.

Barnum watches her with horror as she lays down the curling iron on a metal plate on the table. Now he is sure she's a man.

BARNUM: Did anyone in Europe ever think you was a man?

ZORRO: The crown prince was sure of it.

BARNUM: What happened, if it ain't too personal?

ZORRO: I belted him in the snoot and threw him downstairs.

CUT TO:

91

79   CLOSEUP OF BARNUM: (Shooting So the Bearded Lady Is Reflected in the Mirror)

Barnum has turned away from the looking-glass in despair at this last remark. The Bearded Lady (reflected in the mirror) has put aside her cigar and is bending over—one foot on a chair—lacing her high-topped fancy boots. The Lady's hips are eloquent with rotundity. Barnum turns as though to speak again, when he sees the vision in the mirror. He shows astonishment. Then his face lights up.

CUT TO:

80   INTERIOR: Bearded Lady's Dressing Room— Another Angle

Showing Barnum surveying the bulging stern with joy born of a home run in the ninth. He edges behind her cautiously, starts past, just letting his hand brush the billows. He is enraptured. She jumps a little.

ZORRO *her alfalfa oscillating:* Why, Phineas....

Mr. Barnum flushes like a grand slam in hearts.

BARNUM: I didn't mean nothin'....

ZORRO *shaking a finger and baby talking:* Bad, bad boy....

BARNUM: Nice weather we been having....

As she advances on him—a poor, love-starved

92

wench, he amends hastily: But it looks like rain.
...*Getting ready to duck:* Gotta go see if them
tarpaulins is over the—

ZORRO *catching hold of his hand:* This is the
first time we've had to get acquainted, Phineas....
Let's sit down and talk.

BARNUM *swallowing—an apprehensive eye on
the door:* I'll come back later, an'...

ZORRO *a lady logician:* There's no time like the
present, Phineas....

She drops to the settee abruptly, dragging the astonished Barnum down beside her.

80-A   CLOSEUP OF BARNUM AND ZORRO ON SETTEE

Barnum squirms like a nonplussed sea cow, not knowing whether to make a bolt for the door or to leave it
to the Almighty to extricate him. Zorro is fondling
his hands.

ZORRO *Thais on the make:* You've got such
beautiful hands ...

C U T   T O :

80-B   CLOSEUP OF BARNUM'S HANDS

They are huge, freckled—the skin resembling elephant's hide.

93

ZORRO'S VOICE *continuing:* ...delicate and soft as a baby's....

CUT TO:

80-C CLOSEUP OF BARNUM AND ZORRO ON SETTEE

Barnum is perspiring profusely. He attempts to draw his hands away, succeeds in getting one free, but she clings to the other with a death-grip. Barnum pulls out his watch.

BARNUM *believing himself subtle:* My, my... it's almost five, an'...

ZORRO *ignoring his remark—turns his imprisoned hand palm upward:* What an interesting palm....*Stroking one line in his hand.* You're going far, Phineas... nothing can stop you. I see fortune, fame, riches....*Barnum is beginning to relax, growing interested. Zorro strokes another line in his hand:* That's your love line—it ain't hardly been marked yet. That's strange too, because...*She pinches the flesh of the palm of his hand under the thumb:* ...you're a very romantic man, capable of a grand passion...*She pronounces "grand passion" in the French manner.* ...But wait...*She peers closely at his hand:* ...Here...*She points*...the future holds something in store for you....It's right at your doorstep....*He listens eagerly....* You're going to

94

meet someone—someone who loves and under-
stands you as you've never been understood before.... She's got black hair, Phineas, and—and
hazel eyes—and—and— *Suddenly looking him full
in the face.* Phineas! Are my eyes hazel?

Barnum is suddenly yanked back to earth. He gasps
as he gets the purport of all this—sweats blood.

BARNUM *jittery—stammering:* Don't ask me,
Madame Zorro. I—I'm color-blind.... *Leaping to
his feet....* And now ef you'll excuse me....
ZORRO *clinging to his hand:* Don't leave me,
Phineas ... I'm so lonesome. You don't know how
lonesome I get behind this hedge.... *For the moment she is so tragically wistful that Barnum
swallows uncomfortably. She takes heart at this.*
You think I'm a freak and a curiosity, but I'm a
woman and I'd like to hear the patter of baby
feet, too, or hold a hot iron to a dear husband's
back if he had lumbago. *She gives him a haunted
look, gets to her feet. His horror returns—he tries
to wrench his hand free.* Just holding your hands
like this is like holding onto a burning torch. Just
think how it'd be if you were to put your arms
around me—
BARNUM *outraged—wrenches free:* Stop! I'm a
married man—and besides, I gotta appoint-
ment....

He backs away but she is upon him like a flash, apply-
ing a strangle hold and dusting his horrified jowl with

a Vandyke broom.

> ZORRO *impassioned:* You can't leave me after all the sweet things you've said to me. . . .

Barnum makes one last wrench to free himself, bracing himself on the dressing-room table where rests the still hot curling iron. Barnum sits down on it.

> BARNUM: Jumpin' Jehosophat!

> ZORRO *her ear-drums cracking:* Sweetheart! What have I done?

He leaps like a chamois for the exit, holding his smoking seat.

> ZORRO: Phineas! You can't leave me like this. . . .

She grabs him by the coat tails and starts to pull him back.

C U T   T O :

---

81   INTERIOR: Barnum's Private Office in Museum

Walsh is propped back on his chair, his feet on the desk, teething on a pencil, as the door is flung open and Barnum enters. There is a haunted lustre to his eyes, his hair is standing on end, his hat crumpled in his hand. He is breathless, as one who has run a great distance. He closes the door and makes for the couch, slumping down on it, his glassy eyes staring ceilingward. Walsh watches him in amazement.

96

A gloating impresario, Barnum (Beery), tells his wife (Janet Beecher) of the commercial worth of Josie Heath (Lucille La Verne), George Washington's original nurse.

WALSH: Come, come, P. T. . . . What's the verdict? *As Barnum seems not to hear:* Speak up, man! Speak up!

Slowly Barnum sits up, grips the arm of the couch with one hand, and faces Walsh solemnly.

CUT TO:

---

82   CLOSEUP OF BARNUM

As he eyes Walsh solemnly.

BARNUM: Mr. Walsh, you can tell the WORLD that Madame Zorro is positively a LADY.

FADE OUT.

---

83   EXTERIOR: Barnum's Museum—Closeup of Large Banner Stretched Across Front of Building

---

Which reads:

"SPECIAL ADDED ATTRACTION TODAY. . . . AT TWELVE O'CLOCK NOON. . . . MADAME ZORRO. . . . IS SHE MAN OR IS SHE WOMAN? . . . This international question will be decided today, for once and forever!"

There is also a goodly portrait of the Bearded Lady on the banner—Mona Lisa with a muff.

CAMERA PANS DOWN to show—

97

84 EXTERIOR: Barnum's Museum — Long Shot — Day

The street and sidewalks are crowded with people fighting their way in to buy tickets. Policemen are trying to control the mob. A band is blazing away on the sidewalk.

CUT TO:

85 INTERIOR: Barnum's Museum — Close Shot at Ticket Offices

A swarming mass of people are about the ticket offices. Ellen and the other two girls are trying their best to handle the customers and make change. Walsh is standing beside the ticket office over which Ellen presides. A man is protesting to Ellen.

> MAN: What's the meaning of this? ... Doubling your prices?
> WALSH *stepping up:* Don't you realize, sir, that this is an international event? Three of New York's social leaders as judges! The Honorable Mr. Daniel Webster, in person, acting as stakeholder! *The man is aghast, as Walsh hurries him along:* You're blocking the line, my timid sir.

The man, subdued, purchases his ticket and passes inside. Other customers take his place. Ellen looks wor-

98

shipfully at Walsh, as he makes this oration.

CUT TO:

---

86   EXTERIOR: Street Outside Museum – Long Shot

The populace is yammering like a Moose picnic.

    CROWD *ad libbing:* There's Barnum now! ... Hurrah for Barnum! ... Who's all right? ... Barnum! ... Barnum! ...

A police escort opens the way for the Barnum chariot, which stops at the curbing. Barnum is raising his hat to the public, beaming, while Nancy sits beside him, cringing and detesting the whole thing. She seems somewhat worried. Gendarmes clear the way for the Barnums to alight.

---

87   EXTERIOR: Street Outside Museum – Close Shot at Curb

As Barnum, still tipping his hat, steps out of the carriage.

    BARNUM *to the cheering yokels:* Delighted. ... 'Lo, brother ... thanks. ... Great honor. ... *As he turns with great ceremony to help the frozen-faced Nancy to alight—he speaks in an undertone:* Smile at 'em, Nancy. ...

At this moment a small boy crowds forward, pulls at

99

Barnum's coattails, yells derisively.

> SMALL BOY: My father says you're a big
> fake. . . .

Barnum "takes" this—he would like to garrote the
brat, but he always remembers his public.

> BARNUM *with a beatific smile—placing his*
> *hand on the small boy's head:* I love little
> children. . . .

The crowd applauds, as Barnum, bowing right and
left, starts into the Museum, Nancy following meekly.

CUT TO:

---

88   INTERIOR: Bearded Lady's Dressing Room—
Closeup Bearded Lady (Madame Zorro)

Madame Zorro is standing at one side of the dressing
room, her left foot on a chair, and puffing like a volcano
at a big black cigar. She seems to be deep in con-
templation.

> SKIFF'S VOICE *on* SOUND TRACK: Five hundred
> dollars, Madame Zorro . . .

PULL BACK CAMERA to include Skiff, who is standing
near her.

> ZORRO *haughtily:* You can't bribe me . . . for
> five hundred dollars. . . . I'm a lady.

> SKIFF *the auctioneer:* Seven hundred and
> fifty. . . .

Madame Zorro with supreme contempt moves over to

the door—throws it open—indicating that Skiff get out. She has all the airs of a prima donna. Skiff takes a deep breath.

SKIFF: This is final.... One thousand dollars—cash!

Madame Zorro looks up at him with interest—then deliberately closes the door, starting back to him.

ZORRO *as she moves back to Skiff:* Why didn't you say so—in the first place?

CUT TO:

---

89   INTERIOR: Barnum's Museum—Long Shot

Showing the place filled to capacity. We are SHOOT-ING over the heads of the masses to the platform erected in the background. On the platform are three dowagers, social arbiters... the dignified Mr. Greeley ... Mr. Daniel Webster and Mr. Walsh.... Barnum, very much on his feet, is making a speech.

BARNUM *his voice booming over the crowd:* And so—Ladies and Gentlemun....

---

90   CLOSE SHOT AT PLATFORM—INTERIOR: Barnum's Museum

Showing the group—Barnum in foreground.

BARNUM *continuing:* ... Being as how Mr. Greeley has made the direct challenge, I am here and now accepting it.... *He turns and bows to Mr. Greeley—who sits motionless. There is a round of applause from the crowd:* I take pleasure in introducing to you that great statesman, Mr. Daniel Webster....

There is applause and Barnum signifies that Webster take a bow—which he does against his will.

---

91   CLOSEUP NANCY—in the Audience—INTERIOR: Barnum's Museum

She is cowering against a back wall...ashamed... sick of the whole procedure. She drops her head.

BARNUM'S VOICE *on* SOUND TRACK: Mr. Webster is the most honestest....

---

92   CLOSEUP BARNUM—ON PLATFORM—INTERIOR: Barnum's Museum

BARNUM *waxing eloquent:* ...And patriotic stakeholder that ever lived in America, the home of the free.... *Tremendous applause.* And the three ladies, the cream of New York sassiety....

93   CLOSEUP: Three Dowagers on Platform—
      INTERIOR: Barnum's Museum

They exchange horrified glances.
  BARNUM'S VOICE *on* SOUND TRACK: . . . Whose
  name is a household word. . . .

94   INTERIOR: Barnum's Museum—Close Shot
      at Platform

  BARNUM *continuing:* . . . Mrs.—Mrs. . . . *He*
  founders and finishes quickly to cover up the fact
  that he does not remember their names. Well—
  you all know 'em. . . . *A laugh from crowd.* These
  three ladies whose word is above reproach—are
  going personally to interview Madame Zorro in
  her dressin' room. . . . Followin' which, they will
  then pernounce their verdict. . . .
Applause and hoots from crowd. Barnum is bowing to
Walsh who is already moving over to the ladies to
guide them to the dressing room. As they are being
escorted down the steps by Walsh, Barnum turns to
the band.
  BARNUM: Will the band render us a tune? It
  would be appropriate, seein' as how Madame Zorro
  was born in the South—of England—that the band
  favor us with that great Southern melody,
  "DIXIE!" *Applause—cheers.*

95   INTERIOR: Barnum's Museum—Closeup of Band

Their lungs expanding—as the leader starts the tune "DIXIE."

Cheers, applause, and singing from audience.

CUT TO:

96   INTERIOR: Bearded Lady's Dressing Room— (Madame Zorro's)

Faintly on SOUND TRACK is heard the band playing "DIXIE."

Madame Zorro has disappeared, together with Skiff. But standing before the dressing table, hurriedly getting into her clothes—pulling down her skirts, and pulling a wig over his head, is a strange male citizen. Fortunately Nature has bestowed upon him a luxurious beard.

97   INTERIOR: Barnum's Museum—Long Corridor—Leading to Dressing Rooms

Mr. Walsh, with great ceremony, is escorting the three ladies to the dressing room. He comes up to the door and knocks—then steps back.

     WALSH: Madame Zorro is expecting you.

The three Dowagers, feeling the importance of their position, paradoxically loathing it, and yet with do-or-die expressions on their faces, invade Zorro's dressing room.

WALSH: Tod.... *He takes a few steps forward to meet an attendant.*

---

98   INTERIOR: Barnum's Museum – Another Part of Corridor

Walsh moves briskly in to meet Tod, the attendant shown before.

WALSH *pulling bunch of papers out of pocket:* Take these stories to every paper but Greeley's. ... We'll have headlines ... GREELEY MADE LAUGHING STOCK in every paper! ... This'll TRIPLE our business.

He is interrupted at this moment by screams, horrified yammers, and looks off in direction of the Bearded Lady's Dressing Room.

---

99   INTERIOR: Barnum's Museum – Corridor Outside Madame Zorro's Dressing Room – Close Shot

---

The three scandalized Dowagers are rushing out of the room.

DOWAGERS *ad lib:* I'm going to faint.... How terrible.... I'll never forget this....

---

100   INTERIOR: Barnum's Museum—Long Shot Corridor Outside Madame Zorro's Dressing Room

---

Showing the stunned Walsh in foreground, the outraged Dowagers scuttling toward the Museum in the background.

WALSH *dazed:* Ladies—Ladies ... please.... *He starts after them.*

CUT TO:

---

101   INTERIOR: Barnum's Museum—Close Shot at Platform

The band has stopped playing. Barnum is haranguing the audience.

BARNUM: Ladies and Gentlemen, you will learn once and for all that the name of Barnum is the bullworks of honesty and fair play....

At this juncture, the hyena-yells of the outraged females drown out his sentiments. He turns with an amazed gape and sees—

102   INTERIOR: Barnum's Museum – Flash of the
      Three Fleeing Society Women

As they make way through the populace, toward the
platform.

                                          CUT TO:

103   INTERIOR: Barnum's Museum – Closeup of
      Barnum on Platform

His face has a betrayed, vacuum quality. PULL CAMERA
BACK to show—

104   INTERIOR: Barnum's Museum – Medium Shot
      of Platform

Barnum is still in a fog. Everyone is standing with
mumbling, electrified rigidity, as the three ladies, followed by Walsh, come up to the platform.
      THREE LADIES *in unison, to Barnum:* It's an
      outrage! You impostor! Trying to foist a man off
      as a woman! You ought to be put behind bars!
The brooding silence is broken by one voice.
      VOICE *from audience:* Fake! Barnum's a fake:
                                          CUT TO:

105　INTERIOR: Barnum's Museum—Close Shot of Skiff in Audience

His voice is the spark that sets off the powder.

　　SKIFF *risking the vocal cords:* Tear the place down. Robbing us of our money! Fake!

Others take up the cry.

　　CROWD *ad lib:* A bloated scoundrel! Get a rope! String him up to a rafter! Tear down the place! Fake! Fake! Boo-o-o-o-ooooo.... Sssssssssss!

106　INTERIOR: Barnum's Museum—Long Shot

Purgatory, with a dash of volcanoes. The citizens shriek, curse and bubble with venom.

　　　　　　　　　　　　　　　　　　CUT TO:

107　INTERIOR: Barnum's Museum—Closeup Barnum, Walsh and Greeley

The great showman is flabbergasted. Walsh stands valiantly beside his stricken chief, whose mouth sags with naïve wonderment. Greeley gazes with superiority at the gaping Barnum.

　　BARNUM *rigor mortis setting in:* Somethin's gone wrong....

　　GREELEY: So it seems, Mr. Barnum....

At this strained moment a rotten tomato takes wing and finds a nesting-place in Barnum's eye, Mr. Greeley having leaped aside like a gazelle to escape a fruity fate.

CUT TO:

108   INTERIOR: Barnum's Museum – Close Shot in Midst of Swirling Mob

Fighting and shouting. A small showcase marked "TRAINED FLEAS" is on a dais. A burly citizen picks up this coffin-like receptacle and hurls it with trench-mortar speed in Barnum's direction.

CUT TO:

109   INTERIOR: Barnum's Museum – Close Shot Edge of Platform

Showing Greeley endeavoring to escape from the rostrum, when the case labelled "TRAINED FLEAS" catches him on the back of the skull. The eminent journalist goes down with a hurly-burly bang, his beaver hat sailing off and his walking stick ascending like a rocket.

CUT TO:

110   CLOSE SHOT AT ROW OF EGYPTIAN MUMMIES
      —INTERIOR: Museum

These desiccated mementoes of the Nile's civilization
have been standing upright against the wall. Now people are bowling over the supposed pharaohs, battering
them with vases, cudgels and canes.

                                        CUT TO:

111   INTERIOR: Barnum's   Museum—Closeup
      Greeley on Platform

The leader of the Fourth Estate is just beginning to
come to. Suddenly he sits bolt upright, starting fren-
ziedly to scratch, the "TRAINED FLEA" case on top
of him.

                                        CUT TO:

112   INTERIOR: Barnum's Museum—Long Shot
      Crowd

Still reducing everything in sight.

                                        CUT TO:

113 INTERIOR: Barnum's Museum—Another Section of Museum

Mr. Barnum is fighting his way through the bedlam.
BARNUM: Relax, my friends. Control yourself. . . .
This is a signal for everyone to leap upon the great man. He puts up a game fight against odds.

CUT TO:

114 INTERIOR: Barnum's Museum—Close Shot at Ticket Offices

Showing the mob storming the three ticket booths. A lynching spirit is in the air—also some missiles. Walsh is here—on guard.
WALSH *to the shock troops:* You'll get your money back. Just keep your shirts on.
VOICES OF CROWD: You bet we'll get it back! Hurry up, you perfumed thief! Crooks! Give us our money!

CUT TO:

115 INTERIOR: Barnum's Museum—Close Shot Ellen's Ticket Office

The lass is frantic, trying to make refunds, but the enraged patrons are too much. One colossal broad and her bruiser beau are at the head of a flying wedge. The lady reaches in and grabs a handful of bills from Ellen.

ELLEN *a wounded doe:* Mr. Walsh!

At this Mr. Walsh is into the scene, Sir Galahad to the fore. He quickly relieves the big broad of her hysterical gains as her pugilistic escort goes muscular.

BRUISER: Insult my wife, will yah?

The bruiser starts a swing from the floor, Walsh weaves and bobs and the blow misses him to connect like pay-day at the powder mill, flush on the lassie's chin. She gives a graveyard "Awk!" and collapses amid a fancied twitter of canaries.

CUT TO:

---

116   INTERIOR: Barnum's Museum—Close Shot at Doors Leading into the Museum

---

The police are coming in, clubs in action, to quell the riot.

CUT TO:

---

117   INTERIOR: Museum—Close Shot Group Around Barnum

His noggin is spilling gore, but he still is flailing doggedly, a punch-drunk Horatio at the Bridge.

NANCY'S VOICE *on* SOUND TRACK—*piping above the din:* Phineas! Phin-ee-as ... !

Barnum (Beery) tells his ward, Ellie (Rochelle Hudson),
that he will "give Mr. Walsh (Menjou) the air."

118 INTERIOR: Barnum's Museum—Follow Shot
     of Nancy

Struggling through the crowd, an Amazon on the loose, passing the wall where the various freaks are crouching in terror. As she goes by the platform where the sword-swallower sits, she reaches up and commandeers a sabre from that horrified dietician, and starts, with renewed vigor, to reach Barnum, flourishing the weapon.

NANCY: Out o' my way! I'm warnin' ye, man, woman or child. Let me through!

CUT TO:

119 INTERIOR: Barnum's Museum—Another
     Angle

Depicting Barnum trying fisticuffs with the mob, but being battered down. Nancy comes like an avenging angel, sword aloft.

NANCY: Phineas! I'm here with you.

CUT TO:

120 INTERIOR: Barnum's Museum—Closeup of
     White Cow

Over which is a placard: "SACRED COW OF INDIA." The cow is pulling at the rope, madly fuddled and trying to escape. It finally breaks loose and rushes out.

CUT TO:

121   INTERIOR: Barnum's Museum—Long Shot

Showing everything in a state of chaos—Rome after the vandals have had an inning. People running—the sacred cow mooing and curvetting. Terrified freaks in a panic.

CUT TO:

122   INTERIOR: Barnum's Museum—Close Shot at Ellen's Ticket Office

The mob is stampeding. They now have overpowered Walsh and Ellen. They are helping themselves to the money, while Walsh is protecting the frightened, sobbing girl. Walsh steps on one man's hand, as the latter seeks to pick up a coin from the floor. There is a yowl.

CUT TO:

123   INTERIOR: Barnum's Museum—Medium Shot

Showing a group of policemen fighting their way through, using their billies right and left.

CUT TO:

124 INTERIOR: Barnum's Office—Long Shot

Showing the wrecked Museum and the mad crowd, the smashed exhibits, the rabid cow and the freaks—the policemen working at their sticks.

CUT TO:

125 INTERIOR: Barnum's Museum—Close Shot of Nancy

Fighting among the crowd with her sword. She swings her cutlass until arm weary. Her hat is over one ear, but her spirit is that of a pioneer woman standing off the redskins in the blockhouse.

PAN CAMERA DOWN to show Barnum's head, peering out from under Nancy's skirts. This is his one spot of refuge—Davy Crockett on one knee, taking the count.

DISSOLVE TO:

126 INTERIOR: Barnum's Museum—Long Shot— Day

The place is pulverized and practically deserted. The gendarmes are herding out the last of the sullen and exhausted crowd.

In the background in a small and strained group are

Barnum, Walsh, Nancy and Ellen. CAMERA PANS UP
to a—

---

127   CLOSER SHOT OF THE GROUP INCLUDING
Barnum, Walsh, Nancy and Ellen

CAMERA picks up the ruins as it travels, comes to the
four silent figures. Nancy is seated on a packing box,
her hat still over one eye, worn to a frazzle. She leans
on her sword, like a crutch. Ellen is slumped against
the wall, sobbing in a subdued tone. Walsh is surveying the late field of carnage, a satirical, bitter smile on
his lips. Barnum, hands in pockets, stares down at the
floor, the picture of dejection and despair. No one
moves. No one speaks, as we—

FADE OUT:

FADE IN:

---

128   INTERIOR: Barnum's Bedroom—Closeup of
Nancy—Night

This, of course, is the same house as indicated in the
preceding sequences. The room is groaning with its
weight of walnut furniture. The scene opens with a
CLOSEUP of Nancy on her knees before an open trunk.
The cadaverous alley cat is brushing against her. Once
again Nancy is packing with Connecticut motives and
a grim fervor.

116

CAMERA PANS SWIFTLY to reveal Barnum, lying on the bed, stocking-footed—the Dying Gladiator of the amusement world. On one eye, completely hooding it, is a raw beefsteak. His sigh seems to struggle up from an artesian well. Nancy comes over, the cat following her. The animal scents Mr. Barnum's beefsteak visor.

> NANCY *quivering as she holds up a set of red flannels:* These are full of moths, Phineas.

The animal, seduced by steak, leaps to the bed and advances on the recumbent ex-czar of the freaks.

> BARNUM *a melancholy Cyclops who sees only space:* So's my pore brains.... *The marauding cat is sniffing at the steak:* Git away! Will yah! *He almost weeps with impotence:* Consarn it!

---

129   LONGER SHOT—INTERIOR: Barnum's Bedroom

Nancy starts back to the trunk as Ellen enters the room with some more clothes for Nancy to pack, and she sees poor Barnum's predicament. She shoos the cat off and sits down on the edge of the bed holding Barnum's hand.

> ELLEN: Poor Uncle Phineas....
>
> NANCY *explosively:* He brought it all on hisself....

Barnum groans.

> NANCY *continuing:* It's Divine Providence....

117

He'll HAVE to go back to Connecticut now....
Her voice quivers: ... bein' down and out.

BARNUM *rises up on one elbow:* A Barnum
may be out but never down! ... Stop packin' them
trunks, Nancy....

NANCY *ironically:* Who do you expect to come
to the rescue this time? Your FRIEND Mr. Walsh?
Ellen winces at this.

BARNUM: That's pure sourcasm, Nancy.

NANCY *half-choking in her anger and rage:*
Even Job hisself couldn't of put up with such bitter tests.... Losing the whole four thousand dollars we'd saved up—Mr. Walsh bettin' the
bearded man was a WOMAN.

BARNUM: She was a female of the first water
... and Mr. Walsh didn't bet it.... *I* did! *As
Nancy looks horrified—Barnum continues defiantly:* And what's more I bet all three thousand
of his'n ... and he didn't inch and pinch me....
No, sir! But YOU, the wife of my own bosom,
rises up and stings me like an adder.... You don't
appreciate Mr. Walsh....

NANCY *contemptuously:* I notice he ain't showed
up today....

BARNUM *waxing eloquent:* And why? ... I
betcha—

NANCY *caustically:* You're good with bettin'....

BARNUM *ignoring this:* I betcha he's out formin'
a wonderful plan to help us. I didn't save his brain

118

fur nothin'. . . . There's at least three million cells in that great brain of his that ain't even been touched. . . . They ain't even been extended. . . . *Dramatically:* Mark my words. . . . Nancy . . . he'll bust in here with an idea that'll make you shiver when you hear it. . . .

WALSH'S VOICE *on* SOUND TRACK *yodeling:* Ah-de-lay-he-hoo-o-o-oo!

Every eye goes to the doorway.

---

130   CLOSE SHOT DOORWAY—Leading to Hall— INTERIOR: Barnum's Bedroom

---

Walsh steps inside the door, as drunk as a hoot-owl, but always the gentleman. . . . He carries his hat across his arm—(in the manner of the old-time hoofers).

    WALSH *brightly—attempting the ballet dancer's third position, toe uplifted—but colliding against the door jamb:* Such a happy little family group. . . . *To Nancy:* Hello, gossip.

She gives him a stiletto glare.

---

131   INTERIOR: Barnum's Bedroom—Full Shot

Barnum sits up, completely forgetting the shiner. Ellen is ready to burst into tears, and Nancy has risen and stands motionless, the Avenging Angel at its best.

    BARNUM *hoarsely:* Mr. Walsh . . . say it ain't

so ... tell me my eyes deceive me. ... You ain't ...

WALSH *elfish:* I'm afraid I am. ... Phineas. ... *He hiccoughs:* ... In fact, I'm sure. ...

ELLEN: Mr. Walsh—how could you?

NANCY *her voice dripping ice:* HE can do anything. ...

WALSH *holds out his arms to Nancy:* Shall we tread a measure? *He whistles a few bars and pirouettes.*

NANCY *her eyes glinting steel:* How did you get up here?

WALSH: With the aid of an open window and a little morning-glory vine.

BARNUM *shaking his head:* Mr. Walsh ... I feel jest like someone pulled out a chair from under me. ... My last prop is gone.

NANCY: Phineas Barnum—are you going to stand by and see respectable women insulted?

WALSH *to Nancy:* Virtue affronted. ... *He bows low from the waist and almost topples to the floor.*

WALSH *continuing:* Madam, my sincere apologies ... never again shall a drop of Satan's nectar touch my lips. ... *In the same breath to Barnum:* You haven't by chance a drop of ... hard cider—P. T.?

BARNUM: You've stabbed me in my quick, Mr. Walsh. ...

NANCY *furiously:* Phineas Barnum—if you don't

throw that messenger of the Devil ... outta this house ... *I* will!

WALSH *looking admiringly at Nancy:* Madam, you have missed your vocation ... you would have made an admirable bouncer. ... *Before anyone can answer, he raises his finger lightly and adjusts his hat:* Tcht ... tcht ... I am always the first to take a hint, no matter how slight. ... *He takes off his hat and bows, to both Nancy and Ellen:* Adieu. ...

He starts to the door. Barnum, looking at him sorrowfully, starts after him.

NANCY *sharply:* Mr. Barnum!

BARNUM *from doorway:* I'm jest gonna see he gets out all right. ...

Walsh has disappeared through the door—and Barnum peeks back in the doorway—sorrowfully.

BARNUM: You might as well finish packin', Nancy. ...

As he goes out, Ellen bursts into tears and falls face downward on the bed.

NANCY *firmly:* Save your tears, Ellen. ... He's beyond redemption.

But Ellen continues to sob heartbrokenly.

CUT TO:

121

Barnum is just warping Walsh down the last few stairs.
Walsh, sliding and gliding as he clings to the banister,
is very gay, airy and affectionate.

>WALSH *attempting to cavort:* I'd like to be a
>mountain goat . . . leaping from crag to crag. *He
>yodels:* Ah-de-lay-he-hoo-o-o-oo!

He does a flying leap from the stairs.

>BARNUM *in horror—grabs his legs:* Mr. Walsh!
>WALSH *coyly turns around in Barnum's arms
>and clasps him about the neck:* Phineas, do you
>think it's wrong to kiss a man if you love him?
>BARNUM *trying to escape the kisses:* Control
>yourself, Mr. Walsh. Think what the world would
>say if they seed you upsettin' our dignity.
>WALSH *whooping it up:* I love you, Sir Phineas.
>Understand, milord?
>BARNUM *on guard against further osculation:*
>Please. . . . Exercise some will power.
>WALSH: Why, I'd cut off my right arm for you.
>I only wish I had TWO right arms. Three. An
>octopus. That's it. A loyal, loving octopus. *He
>makes swimming motions like a squid and rolls
>his eyes and snorts:* Whooshee! Whooshee! Nice
>li'l octopus. Whooshee!

He dives out of Barnum's arms and lands on the bottom step, Barnum going down with him.

BARNUM *as he picks himself up—sorrowfully:*
Try and concentrate a little.

At this moment the doorbell rings. Barnum hesitates whether to answer the door, then plops Walsh on the lower step.

BARNUM *whispering:* Be quiet and don't budge.
It may be the Sheriff.

The bell rings again.

WALSH *with a hiccough:* If it's the undertaker, admit him.

BARNUM *as he starts for the front door:* Fate has thrown me to the dogs.

He exits, gloomily.

C U T   T O :

---

133 EXTERIOR: Barnum's House—Close Shot at Front Door

(NOTE: This is a door in two sections, the top and bottom opening independently—an old Dutch Colonial door—so that when Barnum opens the upper half, he is revealed only to the waistline.)

Barnum opens the top half of the door in CAMERA, seems startled to see that no one is there. He looks up and down the street, scowling. He slams the door shut. The SHOT is from Barnum's waist up.

C U T   T O :

134 INTERIOR: Barnum's Lower Hall (Shooting toward Front Door)

Showing Barnum about to turn away from the door, his back to the CAMERA, as the doorbell rings again. He opens the top door again, is looking up and down the street, mystified, when we hear a voice over SOUND TRACK.

> VOICE *over* SOUND TRACK: Are you Mr. Barnum?

Barnum, bewildered, looks round and then down.

CUT TO:

135 EXTERIOR: Barnum's House – Medium Shot at Front Door

Barnum looks down as we PAN TO a midget, who stands not quite up to the top edge of the lower door.

> BARNUM *staring:* Jumpin' Jehosophat! Come in, sir.

He opens the lower door and the midget starts in.

CUT TO:

136 INTERIOR: Hallway Barnum's House

SHOOTING so that Barnum and the midget are in the foreground and Walsh is sprawled out on the bottom stair, his head against the newel post, his eyes closed. The midget is a forlorn little figure. His face is peaked, his clothes shabby and he seems very tired.

> MIDGET *plaintively:* I read your advertisement ... but it took me a month to save up money to git here. ... You see I live in a little town outside Cincinnati ... and if it hadn't been for me being able to ride half fare. ...

Barnum has stood there open-mouthed, but in the background Walsh, disturbed by the voices, starts to awaken.

---

137 CLOSEUP WALSH ON FOOT OF STAIRS—IN-TERIOR: Barnum's Hallway

---

As he opens his eyes, he stares fascinated ... takes another look, a little bewildered.

> WALSH *awestruck:* Phineas ... which one is YOU?

He starts to his feet, gripping the newel post.

---

138 INTERIOR: Barnum's House—Hallway—Medium Shot

Barnum and the midget glance at Walsh as he careens toward them.

> WALSH *to the midget seriously:* How tall? ... I mean ... are you as small as you look to ME?

MIDGET: Twenty-four inches, sir....

Walsh gives a sigh of relief. It is not something that has come out of the neck of a bottle.

WALSH *gripping Barnum:* Phineas—don't you hear! ... You—you Entrepreneur! Five inches shorter than any midget ever exhibited in the world!

BARNUM *dazed:* I'm tryin' to think, Mr. Walsh....

MIDGET *plaintively:* Don't turn me down, Mr. Barnum.... If I don't get this job, I can't ever marry Lavinia....

BARNUM *stunned:* Marry! Who would ... I mean—how would you manage ... ?

WALSH *who has sobered with a wallop:* You're over your head now, Sir Phineas. If you'll allow me? ... *To the midget:* Er—have you a picture of the lucky damsel?

MIDGET *eagerly pulling out a small tintype:* I always carry it next to my heart.

He hands it to Walsh. They peer at it.

CUT TO:

139   CLOSEUP OF TINTYPE

Clutched in the hands of both Barnum and Walsh. It is a picture of the little Lavinia Warren.

BARNUM: Jumpin' Jehosophat! She's a teeny-weeny, too!

---

140   INTERIOR: Barnum's Hallway — Medium Shot

The midget is looking up eagerly.

MIDGET *with pride:* She's smaller'n me!

BARNUM *suddenly taking it big:* They're wuth a gold mine! We'll have a public weddin'... we'll have ...

NANCY'S VOICE: Phin-ee-as....

Nancy appears down the stairway.

NANCY *accusingly:* What's keepin' you, Phineas?

BARNUM *wildly:* A mint! A fortune! *To the midget:* What's your name?

MIDGET: They call me Tom Thumb.

Nancy by this time has reached the foot of the stairs. It is her turn to grip tight to the newel post, as she stares at the midget.

BARNUM *enthusiastically:* Tom Thumb! *Turning to Nancy:* Nancy ... meet General Tom Thumb! He's wuth his weight in gold!

Nancy starts to collapse against the newel post.

NANCY *faintly:* The smellin' salts! Quick!

FADE OUT:

FADE IN:

141   TITLE:

"In the years that followed, the rise of Barnum as an international figure was unprecedented in all the history of the amusement world. The dynamic American drew on the four corners of the earth and its seven seas for new monstrosities. European tours with Tom Thumb brought him fame and fortune. His reception by Queen Victoria and other crowned heads of Europe made his name a household word. The world came to know him as 'The Mighty Barnum.'"

DISSOLVE THROUGH TO:

142   EXTERIOR: Barnum's American Museum—Day

PANNING ON THE SIGN . . . which is between the third and fourth stories of the building and runs across its entire face . . . and which reads . . .

"BARNUM'S AMERICAN MUSEUM"

DISSOLVE TO:

143   EXTERIOR: Barnum's American Museum—Long Shot

Showing the five stories with the outer balconies around

The Bearded Lady (May Boley) goes on the make for Barnum (Beery) after he has asked if she be man or woman.

the second and third stories.

DISSOLVE TO:

---

144 SERIES OF QUICK FLASHES—INTERIOR: Museum

On SOUND TRACK music of bands.

    A. Zebras, camels and ostriches.

    B. The famous original Siamese Twins—Eng and Chang.

    C. "The Great What-Is-It?—Man or Monkey."

    D. Cannibals from Fiji.

    E. Tom Thumb and his wife Lavinia.

    F. The Mermaid.

    G. Albino Family.

    H. Snake Charmer.

    I. Cardiff Giant.

INCLUDED in these SHOTS, vistas of the sweeping stairways, etc.

DISSOLVE TO:

---

145 TITLE:

"Barnum, the Master Showman, loosed rivers of printer's ink to ballyhoo his wonders. Nothing was too difficult for him to tackle, nothing too expensive. And even now, Walsh was in London with instructions to purchase the greatest of all attrac-

129

tions, JUMBO! The idol of England. The largest elephant ever captured by man. Barnum's slogan was: 'NOTHING IS TOO GOOD FOR THE AMERICAN PUBLIC.'"

DISSOLVE THROUGH TO:

---

146   INTERIOR: Barnum's American Museum – Second Floor – Day

---

Showing great stairwell, with a sweep of wide stairs leading up. Off this promenade is the new and giddy office of the Mighty Barnum. This is quite an elaborate set and calls for consultation with the photograph of the original structure's interior. Crowds of awestruck citizens saunter about, inspecting the strange exhibits. The massive door of Barnum's office opens and a very capable young man, a publicity director, comes out, calling to Tod, once Walsh's copyrunner. Tod, also, is a press agent in his own right, dressed to the hilt, alert and bubbling with sophomoric confidence.

>   PUBLICITY MAN *to Tod:* Mr. Barnum wants you right away.

Tod starts forward hastily and enters Barnum's sanctum.

>   TOD *as he exits:* To hear is to obey.

CUT TO:

The furnishings—Barnum at his best. Egypt and Assyria (freely translated by American decorators) have contributed a massive motif to this striking throne-room of the amusement world's caliph. Mirrors are everywhere except on the ceiling. Incense burns from a vessel on his desk, a chalice which seems a cross between Cæsar's helmet and a Pompeian bedpan. An oil portrait of the master standing among his midgets is on one side of the wall facing the desk. A painting of similar size depicting Napoleon—hand as usual exploring his brassière—holds the other flank of the wall. The Barnum desk seems big enough for a chariot race. There are two globes, one terrestrial, the other celestial, on the desk. An imperial canopy drapes the wall to the rear of the great man's throne. The floor is strewn with hides of jungle beasts; stuffed heads peer out from between tall mirrors.

A black man in turban and Indian Prince habiliments —a glassworks diamond on his forehead—stands in butler fashion beside Barnum's chair. The Mighty Barnum's walking stick, with an elephant's head handle in ivory, and his light beaver topper rest on the expansive desk. Mr. Barnum is carrying all the clothing that a tailor could think up. A high stock poultices his Adam's apple.

Ellen, now a girl of about twenty-one—about five years having passed since last we left her in adolescent tears—is in this huge, rococo room. She is standing at a window, looking down at the street. Nancy, a vision in heavy corded silk, a dolman jingling with jet bugle beads, and a beaded hat perched on her dear head, sits stiff and uncompromising in a high-backed chair that may or may not have graced Charlemagne's dining hall. Barnum holds the center of the floor, pacing up and down, his turbaned attendant handing him his walking stick, which he uses to punctuate his remarks.

Two publicity men already are jotting down notes, and the young man who went to summon Tod, and Tod himself enter and join the busy circle.

> BARNUM *expounding at beginning of scene:* I want you boys to fix up a welcomin' celebration at the docks that'll be the most tremenjus triump' in the history of the city. . . . what do I mean? . . . Of America. . . . Hold on . . . of the UNIVERSE! *Alive with ideas and adjectives, he catches sight of Tod coming in:* . . . you can't let no grass grow under your street—as Mr. Walsh, Heaven pertect his stren'th! arrives here early next month. July fift'. . . . *He beams:* Say, that's my birthday! Jumpin' Jupiter, I wish'd it had of been July fourt'. What a double celebration the country and me could have together! *Letting Nature down easy:* Oh, well . . . where was I? Oh, yes. Mr. Walsh, arrives July fift' on the S.S. ATLANTIC . . .

and guess what? *His yes-men stand hemming him in, and eye him for a clue, but give up:* Ha! Hold onto your seats. *Whacking grandly with his cane —then double-crossing his troops with a profound whisper:* He's bringin' JUMBO with him!

The retinue affect various expressions of amazement, after the manner of courtesans sighing and gasping to obliterate the realities of commerce with illusions of true love.

TOD *a boy meant to go far:* Jumpin' Jehosophat, chief!

BARNUM *flattered by such sincere imitation—he nods:* My sentiments exackly, Toddie.

BARNUM *continuing—goes into a Duke of Wellington mood and barks orders:* Now. Arrange to have captive balloons—with "Welcome Jumbo" on the banners—sent up from different parts of the city! Might as well put my pitcher on the sides of the balloons. I want the militia to be there in full force. And the Mayor, of course, to turn over to Jumbo the keys to the city. Don't forget we gotta have the pilin' under the pier reinforced....
As an afterthought: ... take that up with Tammany Hall. The City owes it to the people—can't afford to jepperdize millions of folks' limbs and lives. This Jumbo stands thirty feet high. Think of it! Thirty-four feet high. And weighs thirty tons. Make it thirty-three tons, boys. That's all.
... *As they start to retreat:* Hold on a minute—

He strikes a gong on the wall and two Egyptian ambassadors appear through a mirror-faced door. He addresses the potentates: Give the boys some seegars as they pass out. . . . Everythin' clear now? PUBLICITY MEN *ad lib as they start out:* Yes, Mr. Barnum. Yes, Mr. Barnum. Yes, Mr. Barnum. Yes . . . yes . . . yes . . . yes . . .

The chorus of "yesses" carries over, growing dimmer and dimmer, but to include next scene, as we

CUT TO:

---

148 INTERIOR: Barnum's American Museum Office—Closeup Nancy—in the High-backed Chair

---

She is shaking her head dismally.

NANCY: Where's it all goin' to end?

CAMERA ZOOMS ACROSS TO BARNUM who is standing before a geographical globe. He gives the globe a spin.

BARNUM: There ain't gonna be no end.

---

149 INTERIOR: American Museum—Barnum's Office—Longer Shot

Ellen has turned away from the window to listen.

BARNUM *testily:* Nancy, can't you never get it through your head—your husband's a SUCCESS. He's squattin' on the top of the world. *He taps the globe.*

134

NANCY: The world turns 'round every twenty-four hours.... *Getting to her feet:* You don't even know YET that Mr. Walsh was able to buy Jumbo. ... You don't know....

BARNUM *emphatically:* I DO know Mr. Walsh's never trun me down.... When I deposed him to Africy to get the great "What-is-it" ... didn't he bring 'im back? ... When he went to the Fiji Islands last year—didn't he come home totin' them Cannibals behindst him? He's done what no immortal man could do....

Ellen is getting a glow out of all this.

ELLEN: You gotta admit THAT, Aunt Nancy.

NANCY: I admit NOTHING ... as far as THAT man is concerned.... *To Barnum suddenly:* Has he written you sayin' he HAD Jumbo?

BARNUM *testily:* How COULD a letter from England get here yet? But I know Mr. Walsh.... The papers say he's comin' back on the S.S. ATLANTIC —and he won't come without Jumbo. Why, he's got cart blank to spend whatever he needs ... and besides my cart blank—he's got his brains ... three million cells still untouched.

NANCY *sniffs:* Come on, Ellen ... we'll be late for the Women's Christian Temperance lecture....

Barnum seems suddenly lost in thought. He is pacing the floor, snapping his fingers.

ELLEN: Good-bye, Uncle Phineas.

Barnum does not reply.

135

NANCY *coldly:* Good-bye, Mr. Barnum....

Barnum seems suddenly aroused from a trance. He snaps his fingers with exaltation.

BARNUM: I gotta idea. It beats everything I ever tried.... I'm gonna write to the President of the United States and invite him to be on hand ...to give Jumbo his first bag of peanuts in America!

As Nancy almost swoons on this—Ellen jumps to put her arm about her.

DISSOLVE TO:

---

150   INSERT: Great Banner at the Pier – Day

Displaying the words:

"WELCOME JUMBO."

MUSIC OF BAND PLAYING. Hundreds of steamboats and tug whistles.

---

151   EXTERIOR: Pier – Long Shot – Shooting to-ward Water – Day

---

Waterfront thronged with Sunday sightseers. There is much excitement, the band in full cry ...citizens toting American and Swedish flags ...a rather conglomerate populace, ranging from youth to age, roughnecks to bon tons. A portion of the boat S.S. ATLANTIC, shown as the vessel is warped to the dock. Steamship whistles blowing, etc.

Barnum's ornate carriage drives up and stops. . . . Four
Arabian horses draw this carriage. . . . Nancy is shrinking back in the vehicle. . . . Ellen, lovely, flushed,
dressed in her best bib and tucker, is breathless. Barnum is bowing right and left.

---

1 52   EXTERIOR: Pier — Closeup Carriage

Barnum climbs out first, sweating with excitement.

> BARNUM: Two minutes more and we'd of been
> too late. . . . *Extends his paw to Nancy.*
> NANCY *shakes her head:* Against my will I've
> come this far—but here I sit. Imagine—all this
> sacrilege . . . on the Sabbath day.
> BARNUM: I can't stop to argue. . . . You oughta
> be proud with all the folks devotin' their Sunday
> to see Jumbo. . . .
> NANCY: Have you ever stopped to think—they
> might not ALL be comin' to see Jumbo? *Barnum
> looks pained—shocked:* I read as how Jenny Lind,
> the singer, is on the same boat. . . .
> BARNUM *disgusted:* Hah! A singer! People can
> get all the singin' they want in church. . . . S'pose
> they're comin' HERE to see one? *Dolefully:* Nancy,
> sometimes you get me worryin' that your mind
> ain't quite sound. . . .

A blast of the boat whistle. Barnum leaps, and without a word starts out.

I 37

ELLEN *climbing over Nancy:* Wait, Uncle
Phineas—I'm coming. . . .
She starts blindly out after the fleeing Barnum.

---

153   FOLLOW SHOT: Barnum Going through
Crowd at Pier

He is puffing, perspiring. He bumps into James Gordon
Greeley, who is in his way. Greeley turns around to
denounce this "shoving person" when Barnum recog-
nizes him.
BARNUM *effusively:* Sure nice of YOU, Mr. Gree-
ley, comin' down to greet Jumbo.
GREELEY *with acid reaction:* Sorry to disillu-
sion you, Barnum. But most of us are here to
meet someone greater than—an elephant.
BARNUM: There ain't NOTHIN' bigger than
Jumbo.
GREELEY: To YOUR way of thinking . . . the
famous Jenny Lind would get second billing to
your Jumbo.
BARNUM: I wouldn't give her house room.
Barnum starts elbowing his way through the crowds.

---

154   CLOSER SHOT: Edge of Pier

This is about the spot where the gangplank will come
down. The longshoremen are tying up the boat, and

138

the sailors are getting ready to lower the gangplank. Ellen is standing there, looking up at the deck, glassy-eyed, as Barnum fights his way through.

BARNUM *excitedly to Ellen:* Pray it don't sink afore they get Jumbo off.... Where's Mr. Walsh? *Looking up toward the top deck—suddenly espies him—out of scene:* There he is. Mr. Walsh! Yoo-hoo—it's me! Phineas! Your P. T.!

---

155 EXTERIOR: Upper Deck of the *S.S. Atlantic*

Walsh, the glass of fashion, raises a conservative hand of greeting.

On SOUND TRACK—cheers—boat whistles—bands.

---

156 EXTERIOR: Pier—Closeup of Barnum and Ellen

Suggestion of surging crowds pushing them. Barnum is so flub-dubby that he can't stand still.

BARNUM *excitedly:* Why didn't he git Jumbo out on deck? Where's the Mayor ...? Listen to 'em, Ellie! *Refers to the shouting, drums, whistling, and cheers:* All for Jumbo! It's tremenjus!

At this moment the sailors let down the gangplank, and before the mariners can stop him, or the mate can come down the gangplank, Barnum rushes up, pushing aside anyone who tries to interfere. He is like a bull charging a red flag.

157   FLASH: Crowds on Pier

As they set up a terrific roar—surge forward.

158   EXTERIOR: Deck of Ship—Close Shot of Walsh

Waiting to go ashore. Barnum dashes up and pumps his hand.

BARNUM: So glad! So glad! Happy to see you back, messmate. So relieved. *Walsh smiles, but before he can say anything, Barnum is all business:* We'll unload him right here. Right here. *Pointing over the edge:* With giant booms and chains.... The band'll play the English National Anthem. *He bursts into the "Marseillaise":* Tum. Tum. Tum-tum-tum-tum-te-ta. *He pulls up short:* I forget how she goes. Anyway it's my idea to keep him from gettin' homesick. NEZ PAH? *Walsh is bewildered as Barnum talks. Barnum yanks Walsh's sleeve:* Don't dawdle, Mr. Walsh. The crowd's impatient to see him.

WALSH: You're talking in circles, P. T. See who?

BARNUM: You ain't been drinkin'? *He sniffs of his breath:* Jumbo, of course.

WALSH: Jumbo? I couldn't get him. The London

Zoo refused to part with Jumbo!

BARNUM *stunned:* You couldn't get...? You're teasin' me, a course, Mr. Walsh. *Laughs hollowly:* A course you got Jumbo.... You ain't never failed me yet.

WALSH: I don't think I've failed you this time. ...Phineas.

BARNUM *desperate:* Will you please to make yourself more plainer, Mr. Walsh.... One minute you say you ain't got Jumbo—and the next minute you say you have....

WALSH *taking Barnum by the coat lapel:* Calm yourself, P. T....Listen.... I DIDN'T BRING BACK JUMBO.... *Barnum closes his eyes as though he were about to swoon:* ...but I did bring something that so far surpasses Jumbo...that...

BARNUM: You coulda brung Napoleon hisself ...and it wouldn't mean nothin' to me.

WALSH: You'll change your mind, Phineas....

BARNUM: I ain't even interested.... What is it?

WALSH: The Swedish Nightingale.

BARNUM: A nightingale! What's happened to your brains...? I give you full leeway, cart blank—and look what you bring back. Who's gonna pay money to see a moulting little bird? Why I got a 'Merican eagle—the BIGGEST bird in the world already.... *Groans:* The 'Merican public likes to be humbugged—but there's a limit....

At this moment, on SOUND TRACK, we hear the voice

of Jenny Lind. She is singing the song Nancy used to slay: *Believe Me If All Those Endearing Young Charms*. Barnum looks startled.

  WALSH: THAT'S Jenny Lind. *He points to the bow of the boat. Barnum stares:* The Swedish Nightingale! The Queen of Song. She's yours.

C U T T O :

159 EXTERIOR: Bow of Ship — Close Shot of Jenny Lind

Standing with arms outstretched, singing to the public below. She is lovely to look upon.

C U T T O :

160 EXTERIOR: Pier — Medium Shot of Crowd on Dock

Listening to the voice which comes over SOUND TRACK. Everyone is standing motionless, staring, entranced.

C U T T O :

161 CLOSEUP OF BARNUM AND WALSH ON DECK

Walsh is looking off in Jenny Lind's direction, but in his eyes there is more than admiration for her warblings. Barnum stands as open-mouthed as a beached halibut.

Jenny Lind's voice comes over SOUND TRACK during
this shot.

> BARNUM *goaled:* That's Nancy's piece. . . . It
> don't seem possible for the same song to come
> outta two mouths so different.

Walsh pays no attention to him. The song reaches its
end.

CUT TO:

---

162   EXTERIOR: Pier – Medium Shot of Crowd on
Dock

As they start to cheer.

> CROWD *ad lib:* Hooray! Bravo! Bis! Throw us
> a kiss, Jenny.

The waterfront début is a triumph.

CUT TO:

---

163   EXTERIOR: Bow of Ship – Close Shot of
Group about Jenny Lind

She is bowing with Nordic charm and flinging kisses
to the cheering public as Walsh comes to her. Barnum,
like a scow in tow, is in Walsh's wake. Lind turns to
Walsh, and her eyes light. He is moon-struck and
adoring.

> WALSH *to Lind:* MIN KARA, may I present to you
> the one and only Barnum. . . .

143

BARNUM *rocked to the heels:* Madame Lind, you're wuth your weight in gold.

LIND: *Très charmante. . . . To Walsh:* Ees he not a most wonnerful impresario?

Barnum is fascinated but slightly dazed. Lind turns to respond again to the cheering throng. Barnum consults his oracle.

BARNUM *in an undertone to Walsh:* What'd she call me?

WALSH *to Barnum:* Impresario? . . . Very flattering. The power behind the throne. *To Lind, who has turned back to them:* Shall we go ashore?

LIND: La . . . yes . . .

She is about to take Walsh's arm, but Barnum, with much dignity, offers her his wing. She hesitates, looks at Walsh.

WALSH: I must defer. We must make up to Phineas for not leading an elephant ashore.

Lind laughs. Barnum is annoyed.

BARNUM: What did you have to say THAT for, Mr. Walsh?

They start out of scene.

CUT TO:

---

164   EXTERIOR: Pier – Foot of Gangplank – Close-up of Ellen

She looks up tremblingly. Her beloved will be with her in a trice.

An enraged public wrecks Barnum's first museum after a committee of society women have proclaimed the "Bearded Lady" a fake.

PULL CAMERA BACK to show the rest of the group about Ellen, including the eager Mr. Greeley. He is puzzled as he sees—

CUT TO:

165   EXTERIOR: Gangplank – Medium Shot

Peacock Barnum is bringing Jenny Lind down the gangplank, Walsh directly behind them.

CUT TO:

166   EXTERIOR: Pier – Foot of Gangplank

The crowd sweeps in as Lind, on Barnum's arm, reaches them. Behind the showman and his new-found treasure comes Walsh. Greeley presses forward, but on seeing Barnum is fuddled.

> BARNUM *to Greeley—with a gloat:* Kinda fooled you, eh, Brother Greeley? *To his songbird, with guffaws:* I had him and the public thinkin' I was importin' an elefunt....*Points to the throng:* That's what brung 'em all here....

Walsh gives Barnum a boot from behind as Lind looks startled and then annoyed. Barnum gazes back, aggrieved.

> WALSH: His Honor, the Mayor, is waiting to extend greetings.

> BARNUM *starting to lead Lind off—speaks to*

Walsh: Won't HE be confused when he finds it ain't Jumbo!

Walsh remains behind, stewing. He removes his topper and dabs at his brow with a kerchief. The rest of the people trail after Barnum and Lind. Only Ellen is left. She looks up eagerly at Walsh, who has not seen her.

ELLEN: Mr. Walsh. . . .

WALSH *he is jerked back to earth:* Why, Ellie! You've grown up. . . .

She smiles uncertainly; then nods off in direction of Lind.

ELLEN: Is she . . . is she going to work for Uncle Phineas?

WALSH: I imagine it will be the other way around.

ELLEN *it's over her head:* She—she's kind of pretty, isn't she?

WALSH *looking after Lind:* KIND of? She's glorious! Face, voice, soul! *In a hurricane:* Heaven's masterpiece! *After his emotional storm subsides:* Pardon me, Ellie. Have to keep an eye on Uncle Phineas.

He starts out of scene. Ellen looks after him, a slaughtered lamb. Her lip does a St. Vitus' fandango, as she starts slowly out of scene.

CUT TO:

She is still staring off, somewhat troubled, toward the group around Lind. Ellen comes into scene and stumbles into the carriage. She sits down limply. Nancy turns and sees her tear-dripping face. She says nothing, but reaches over and pats the girl's hand. The footman comes into the scene.

> FOOTMAN *to Nancy:* Mr. Barnum says we is to go home. He's takin' the lady to the Irving Hotel.

Nancy nods grimly. The footman gets aboard the seat.

> NANCY *in prophetic tone:* Punishment is meted out to them that desecrate the Sabbath day!

The carriage starts out. We hear the cheers and shouts of the crowd and the band playing.

CUT TO:

168   EXTERIOR: Pier—Close Shot at Group

Showing Barnum and Lind. She is clamped in the vise of his elbow. Walsh is on the opposite side of the great man. The Mayor, Greeley and others are gathered close about them. Barnum is looking down at Lind fatuously, a boy longing to cut the birthday cake.

> BARNUM: No foolin'. This country loves Swedes to death.... *To the crowd:* Three rousin' cheers for Madame Lind—*He leads the cheers and the*

crowds burst their lungs following him.

DISSOLVE TO:

169   INSERT — NEWSPAPER

"JENNY LIND DÉBUT
AT CASTLE GARDEN
A MUSICAL THRILL

"Music lovers of New York gathered in great numbers last night at Castle Garden to welcome Mme. Jenny Lind, the Swedish Nightingale, to the concert halls of America. It was a triumph for the noted European songstress and for Mr. Phineas T. Barnum, her manager. Encore after encore was demanded and graciously given, and at the close of the gala occasion the singer seemed flushed and happy. Mr. Barnum, too, was happy —although not flushed. Critics were unanimous that America has at last been visited by one of the truly great artists of all time. Mme. Lind's rendition of the 'Casta Diva' ..."

DISSOLVE TO:

170   NEWSPAPER INSERT:

"MORE TRIUMPHS FOR LIND

"Broadway was jammed yesterday when Mme. Lind emerged from her sixth concert under the management of Phineas T. Barnum. As she left

148

Castle Garden, she was besieged by college boys on vacation from Princeton University. They unhitched the horses of her carriage, and while Mr. Barnum protested, the boys put themselves in harness. Cries of 'Vive, Mme. Lind' were taken up. Mr. Barnum, for some curious reason, thought the word 'Vive' implied some sort of insult, and only after a captain of police, who is of French descent, explained what it meant did Mr. Barnum stop laying about the crowd with his heavy cane. This concert was merely another manifestation of the lady's great charm and artistic power."

Under these newspaper inserts a SERIES of FLASH DISSOLVES.

---

171   FLASH: Full Figure Shot of Lind—Night

Just finishing last three or four bars of opera "NORMA" (or other opera). Huge bouquets are pelted at her as she bows.

     CROWD *cheering ad lib:* Bravo! Encore! Bis! Lind!   DISSOLVE TO:

---

172   FLASH: Closeup Heads of Two or Three Society People

Two can be the women who judged the bearded lady, and Mr. Astor. They are in evening clothes.

149

VOICES OF SOCIETY PEOPLE *ad lib:* Divine!
What an artiste! Lind is marvelous!

DISSOLVE TO:

---

173   MONTAGE SHOTS — CLOSEUP SEVERAL HEADS

Flashed one right after the other. An elderly woman
... an Italian laborer ... a middle-class man ... a
young blood ... Greeley.

> OLD LADY: She brings tears to my heart.
> ITALIAN LABORER: DIO MIO ... BRAVISSIMA!
> MIDDLE-CLASS MAN: I only wish I was young
> again.
> YOUNG BLOOD: What a woman!
> GREELEY: There will never be another Jenny
> Lind.

DISSOLVE TO:

---

174   FLASH — EXTERIOR: Street — Follow Shot —
Night

Men in dress clothes and toppers are pulling Lind's
carriage. Lind is standing up blowing kisses.

> VOICES OF CROWD *ad lib:* Hurrah for Lind!
> Lovely Jenny! A song bird from heaven!

DISSOLVE TO:

150

175   INTERIOR: Barnum's Bedroom in the Oriental Villa—Late Afternoon

ANGLE showing a section of the bedroom. On SOUND TRACK, we hear the gorilla basso profundo of Barnum, picking up the song *Believe Me If All Those Endearing Young Charms*. We also hear the slapping of hands upon human meat. CAMERA PANS OVER to show—

176   INTERIOR: Barnum's Oriental Villa—Barnum's Bedroom—Close Shot of Barnum and Masseur

Mr. Barnum is on his back, gracing a table. A Swedish massage artist is thwacking his torso—a voodoo priest with an obese drum. This manipulation, naturally, does a bit of havoc with the Barnum warbling.

BARNUM *breaking off the aria as he recalls something:* How do you say it again, Ole?

OLE *stolidly:* Lie quiet.

BARNUM *in a sheep's day-dream:* You are very beautiful.... *Ole looks at him, alarmed and entirely suspicious.* Not YOU! How do you say it in Swedish?

OLE *relieved but unemotional:* DU AR GANSKA VACKER.

BARNUM: DU...AR...GANSKA....*He breaks*

off as Ole gives him a battering-ram shove in the
belly. Barnum grabs his stomach: Jehosophat!
OLE *a stoic:* No use. It'll not come off. Like a fat
old woman, you must wear a corset.
BARNUM *is dismayed:* A corset! Over my dead
body, Ole. . . . Uh, uh. It wouldn't be dignified.

DISSOLVE TO:

---

177 INTERIOR: Barnum's Oriental Villa – Barnum's Bedroom – Early Night – Closeup of
Ole

Playing tug-o'-war with strings.

OLE *in a sweat:* Now hold your breath and suck
in your belly.

PULL CAMERA BACK to show Barnum gripping the bureau, purpling and straining, wheezing and gagging as
Ole pulls the strings of a corset which encircles the
great man's midriff. Barnum's eyes are focused on a
picture of Jenny Lind, which rests on the bureau. He
indicates heroically to Ole to pull tighter. Ole obeys,
but as he does so, the strings break and Ole executes
a fantastic buttock-breaker to the opposite side of the
torture chamber.

DISSOLVE TO:

178   INTERIOR: Drawing Room—Barnum's Oriental Villa—Night

In the background is the huge sweeping stairway swirling down into the hall. The room is fearful and wonderful—a miracle of the times. (Follow motif of photograph of the "Vanderbilt residence," filled with gingerbread woodwork, heavy tapestries, plush "suites," white marble statues.)

Ellen is seated at the square piano playing mournfully *Believe Me If All Those Endearing Young Charms*. Nancy is sitting before a small easel working on a sampler, "GOD BLESS OUR HOME," when Barnum starts down the stairway at the back.

RUN CAMERA UP TO: FOOT OF STAIRWAY—showing Barnum, a nightmare of elegance. He affects a monocle and is something to look upon, his corseted figure adorned in evening clothes. He wears a boutonnière. Two valets walk behind him, one carefully brushing off the "topper," and the other carrying Barnum's Inverness cape and his gold-knobbed stick.

179   INTERIOR: Barnum's Oriental Villa—Drawing Room—Closeup Nancy

As she looks up startled, her face drops.
    NANCY: You ain't goin' OUT to supper tonight, are you, Phineas?

153

180 INTERIOR: Drawing Room—Barnum's Oriental Villa—Longer Shot

Ellen turns, startled, from the piano.

BARNUM *trying to maneuver the monocle:* Have you forgot this is the night I give the big banquet for Miss Lind? Everyone's gonna be there ... Mr. Greeley, the poet, Longfeller—the Astors....

NANCY: Oh-h.

BARNUM: You just musta forgot....

NANCY *with a little flash of spirit:* How can I forget something I didn't know....

BARNUM *testily:* Don't say that. I distinkly remember askin' yuh to go ... and you said ... I forgit what your excuse was....

At this moment the monocle drops out of his eye. A servant stoops to retrieve it, but Barnum waves him aside, putting his foot on the monocle, and taking another from his breast pocket.

BARNUM *continuing:* I always tote some extreys along in case.... *He adjusts the monocle to his eye.*

NANCY *who has been looking at him steadily, speaks in a still, dead voice:* You DIDN'T ask me to go, Phineas Barnum ... and yuh know it.... You never ask me to go anywhere ... no more....

BARNUM: That's not fair, Nancy.... After you refusin' to meet Madame Lind.

154

NANCY: I didn't refuse to meet her.

BARNUM: Well, I knew yuh didn't WANT to. . . .
And then about tonight. . . .

NANCY *quietly:* I'd like to be with yuh tonight
. . . Phineas.

BARNUM: Aw, Nancy, you wouldn't like it. . . .
Champagne drinkin' and all them monkeyshines.

ELLEN *impulsively:* Uncle Phineas—take Aunt
Nancy with you tonight. . . . Why. . . . It's your. . . .

NANCY *in steely tones:* Be quiet, child! *Then to
Barnum:* You and me've grown pretty far apart,
Phineas. . . . It was bad enough before SHE came
. . . but now . . . you're under some evil spell.

BARNUM: Aw, Nancy . . . *he starts to her:* . . .
Don't make such a fuss about tonight. . . . It ain't
no different than any other night and . . .

Nancy chokes, a hard, dry sob. Barnum is about to put
his arm about her, when there is a commotion from the
hall.

TOM THUMB'S VOICE *above all others:* I tell
you we're going to see Mr. Barnum . . . tonight!

Barnum whirls about, startled, looking toward the door.

---

181   Another Angle—Drawing Room—Shooting
to the Door Leading to the Hall

Tom Thumb stalks in, followed by Lavinia. Behind
towers the Cardiff Giant, the Siamese twins, the fat
lady.

TOM THUMB: Good evening, Mr. Barnum. . . .

He is nettled.

BARNUM: What you doin' here, General? Why ain't you all at the Museum?

183   Another Angle – Barnum's Drawing Room

Tom Thumb steps ahead of the others, acting as their spokesman.

TOM THUMB *bitterly:* I guess the Museum can get along without us. . . . There ain't enough people come in—to matter.

NANCY *apprehensively:* Why didn't you tell me business was bad, Phineas?

TOM THUMB: Because he didn't know, Mrs. Barnum . . . or didn't care. . . . He hasn't been near the Museum since that great ARTISTE— MADAME LIND—got here. . . .

BARNUM: You leave her name out of it! *Nancy looks curiously and with sudden understanding at Barnum.* Darin' to mention a freak and a wonderful artist in the same breath. . . . It's—it's sacrilege, that's what it is. . . . Now git back where you belong . . . in a museum!

NANCY: Don't talk like that to Tom. . . . Think

156

where we'd be if it hadn't been for Tom. . . .

BARNUM: I'm thinkin' where I'll be—if I stick to 'em! I'm a impresario now—freaks don't interest me. . . . In fact, I'm thinkin' of closin' up the whole shebang. . . .

TOM THUMB: You can't mean that, Mr. Barnum. . . . You can't mean you'd close the Museum. . . .

BARNUM: I'll show you whether I can or not. . . . I ain't got my heart in it—and what I ain't got my heart in—don't succeed. . . .

TOM THUMB: Some day you're going to eat those words, Mr. Barnum. You belong with us and some day you'll realize it.

BARNUM: I've outgrown you—that's what I have. . . . I got culture. . . . I'm a patron of the Arts. . . . Even Mr. Greeley says so. . . . I don't want to be bothered with you no more. . . . Mr. Walsh'll see about your contracts. *To the butler standing in the door:* Isaiah, show these people the way out. . . . *To the one valet who is brushing his topper:* Ezekiel—my tile!

As the valet hands him his hat, Nancy stands motionless watching him. Even Ellen is looking at him as though he were a stranger. In background Tom Thumb turns wearily to the hall door, the others start to follow.

184 INTERIOR: Barnum's Oriental Villa – Medium Shot Hallway

The butler is holding open the door, and Tom Thumb, taking Lavinia's arm, moves out with dignity. The others, following, are crestfallen.

185 INTERIOR: Barnum's Oriental Villa – Drawing Room

Barnum has on his hat and is holding out his arms for the valet to drop the Inverness cape over his shoulders. He feels the tension in the room, sees Nancy's stony-cold face, and begins to feel uneasy.

BARNUM *trying to alibi—the martyr:* They made my blood boil—'specially when they mentioned that lovely goddess—Madame Lind. . . . Why, no man's good enough to kiss the hem of her garment—let alone TALK aboot her. . . .

His conscience stirs him for the moment. He manufactures a smile for Nancy and moves over to her, kissing her hand. . . . She stands like one turned to marble.

BARNUM *jauntily:* ADIR. *He starts to the hall door—throwing back over his shoulder:* That's "good-bye" . . . in Swedish.

He starts out of the door into the hall and Nancy stands

158

motionless until the great hall door is closed. Ellen is looking at her apprehensively and sympathetically.

CUT TO:

---

186   INTERIOR: Barnum's Oriental Villa — Close Shot Nancy

Showing sampler work "GOD BLESS OUR HOME."
She stands motionless, then her knees seem to give way and she sits down. Ellen comes over to her, puts her hand on Nancy's shoulder, but Nancy seems not to be aware of it.

> NANCY *looking into space:* That's the first time he ever forgot.... Today's our weddin' anniversary.

DISSOLVE TO:

---

187   INSERT: Closeup Nancy's Hand Writing a Letter

The same spidery scrawl as before. It reads:
> "I'm going back to where I belong. I realize that you've out-grown me just as you have out-grown other friends."

Ellen's voice comes over SOUND TRACK.

> ELLEN'S VOICE *on* SOUND TRACK: Aunt Nancy....

CUT TO:

159

188 INTERIOR: Drawing Room—Barnum's Oriental Villa—Close Shot at Desk—Night

Nancy, dressed for travel, is at the desk in the room. Nancy glances over the letter and puts it in an envelope. Then she begins heating some sealing wax at a taper.

189 INTERIOR: Drawing Room—Barnum's Oriental Villa—Longer Shot

Ellen, also dressed for traveling, comes down the stairs and into the room. Ellen is carrying a small suitcase. Wordlessly, Nancy affixes the wax and stamps it with a seal. She lays down the letter on the desk, rises, takes one last look about the room, and squares her shoulders.
  NANCY: I'm ready.
She starts out of the room, chin up.

DISSOLVE TO:

190 INTERIOR: Living Room in Jenny Lind's Hotel Suite—Night

Walsh, in evening dress, is sitting at the piano, improvising. We hear Lind's voice from adjoining room where she is dressing, singing snatches of song.
  LIND'S VOICE *from next room:* MIN KARA, play again that leetle strain from "Don Giovanni."

160

The budding showman, Barnum (Wallace Beery), encounters Tom Thumb (George Brasno) for the first time.

WALSH *quizzically, but tenderly:* Are you prac-
tising, MIN ELSKADE, or dressing?

CUT TO:

---

191   INTERIOR: Jenny Lind's Bedroom in Hotel
Suite

Lind, charming and lovely, is sitting before a mirrored
dressing table in a frothy, white negligée. She pats
powder on her nose as her maid arranges her hair. She
is gazing on her own reflection in the mirror, as she
calls out to Walsh in the next room.

LIND *to Walsh:* A leetle of both, my dar-leeng.
Pause. Lees-ten . . . I have a wonderful plan for
tonight. . . .

CUT TO:

---

192   INTERIOR: Living Room in Jenny Lind's
Hotel Suite

Walsh is at the piano.

WALSH: I know . . . you've suddenly developed
tonsilitis, and will be unable to attend the banquet.
Lind appears in the doorway, a mischievous smile on
her lips.

LIND: How could you possib-lee know?
Walsh gets up from the piano and comes over to her.

WALSH *firmly:* You may develop leprosy, smallpox or the mumps, but you're not going to let poor

old P. T. down tonight.

LIND *pouting charmingly:* Bull-ee. . . .

At this moment there is a knock at the door. She turns and flies back into her bedroom. Walsh goes over and opens the door. He steps back, amazed.

CUT TO:

193   INTERIOR: Hotel Corridor (Outside Lind's Door)

Barnum stands there with a proud smile. Two bellboys are bearing a huge horseshoe floral piece of orchids, with Lind's name worked in flowers.

BARNUM: 'Lo, Mr. Walsh. . . . *To bellboys:* Bring it right in, boys.

CUT TO:

194   INTERIOR: Living Room in Jenny Lind's Hotel Suite

Barnum, proud of his achievement, superintends the placing of the floral offering. Walsh looks on, somewhat aghast.

BARNUM *proudly:* What do you think of it?

WALSH *cocks his head to one side as he surveys it—quizzically:* Merely a suggestion, Phineas . . . *lowering his voice:* . . . but you don't suppose Madame Lind will mistake it for a funeral offering?

The two bellboys have gone out of the room.

BARNUM *solemnly:* How could she? There ain't no "Rest in Peace" on it. *A small boy:* Where is she? I can't wait to see her blessed face when she gets a look at this.

WALSH: Neither can I, Phineas.

BARNUM *in a whisper—pointing to a little golden box attached to the offering:* Do you know what's in that box, Mr. Walsh? *As Walsh shakes his head, bewildered:* Ants' eggs!

WALSH *his millions of brain cells reel:* Phineas, do I understand you aright? Ants' eggs?

BARNUM *proudly:* My own idea. . . . Ants' eggs —food for nightingales . . . the Swedish Nightingale. . . . Catch on?

WALSH: Vaguely. . . .

LIND'S VOICE *from next room:* Min elskade. . . . *Barnum turns adoringly—love's fever getting hold:* I have now a wonderful new plan for tonight. . . .

WALSH *coughing in embarrassment:* . . . Er—Mr. Barnum is out here. . . .

LIND'S VOICE *expressive:* Oh. . . .

BARNUM *calls off:* I've come to escort you downstairs in person, Madamwaselle Lind. . . . *No answer—Barnum puts on more steam:* I say, I've—

WALSH *with a bit of bite:* Louder.

BARNUM *sort of hurt:* That's kinda unpolite to an old friend, ain't it?

WALSH: She's not exactly deaf.

BARNUM: What if she was deef? I'd still yell it from the rooftops how I worship her.

WALSH: Shhh-h-h!

BARNUM: Don't shush ME! Ever since I first laid eyes on her. . . .

WALSH *stunned:* Barnum, are you out of your mind?

BARNUM: Let's not discuss. I'm still a young man.

WALSH: P. T.! Wake up. . . . If I'd had the slightest hint. . . . *He grabs Barnum's arms.* Now you listen to me. Forget it—forget all about it. Your contract with Madame Lind expires next week. She'll be going back to Sweden, and . . .

BARNUM: Just leggo. She ain't goin' back to no Swedens. Just wait till I tell her I've took a long term lease on the Temple of Music.

WALSH *groans:* What!

BARNUM: I had to mortgage everything I got,— Museum, the house, EVERYTHING. But . . . *he gestures toward Lind's bedroom* . . . nothin's too good for my little song goddess.

WALSH: Why did you do it? Oh, Phineas!

At this moment there is a rap at the door. Walsh is too overcome to speak or move, but Barnum calls out.

BARNUM *calling:* Come in. . . .

The door opens, and a frenzied maître d'hôtel, flanked by a pair of neurotic waiters, comes in.

164

MAÎTRE D'HÔTEL *surviving an attack of angina pectoris:* MON DIEU, Monsieur Barnum! It has happened, just like I warned you.

BARNUM: What? The partridges?

MAÎTRE D'HÔTEL: The cake! The beeg cake! He collapse like.... *He gestures a big tragedy.* Pouf!

BARNUM: It couldn't of! Why, I won't let it! It was gonna be the piece—the piece—*he looks at Walsh, wild-eyed, for the word.*

WALSH *automatically:* Pièce de résistance.

BARNUM *nodding—to Walsh:* The cake was six feet high, made like a nightingale....

MAÎTRE D'HÔTEL *in broken French:* I warned you.... The body was too heavy for the legs. It went over—so.... *He gestures, as one diving headfirst.*

BARNUM *wildly:* Somethin's GOTTA be done! Make me another cake....

MAÎTRE D'HÔTEL: Eemposseeble.... Eeet is too late.

BARNUM *the czar:* Nothing is impossible! I'll go down and cook it myself. We'll have another cake if it costs me a thousand dollars!

He starts out of the room on the run, followed by the frenzied maître d'hôtel and the waiters. Walsh sighs wearily, as he closes the door after them. He leans against it weakly, then looks off.

C U T T O :

195   INTERIOR: Living Room in Jenny Lind's
       Suite – Close Shot at Doorway Leading to
       Bedroom

Lind, who has finished dressing, is standing there, in
a lovely evening gown, looking at Walsh.

LIND: Now what you theenk? *She nods.* Yes. I
hear all the beeg bool say. *She makes horns at her
forehead.*

CUT TO:

196   INTERIOR: Drawing Room in Jenny Lind's
       Hotel Suite – Longer Shot

The diva stands in the doorway. Walsh walks over to
her, running his hand through his hair. He is weary
and distrait.

WALSH: I never should have quit drinking.

LIND: Eet is all your fault. For you I am nize
to heem. Make smiles at heem. Bah! I work no
longer for the beeg, ree-diculous, stupid orang-
otang!

WALSH *quietly defending P. T.:* Ridiculous
sometimes, ELSKLING. But never stupid.

LIND *fuming:* No? I suppose he feets in a royal
court? With queens?

WALSH: A queen HAS received him, ELSKLING.
A very great and kindly lady—Victoria. Perhaps

she was amused at first, but the Court saw beyond
the crudities and the noise; saw something real
and great inside the man, something bigger than
social gestures, nobler than polished manners.
Lind sniffs disgustedly.

LIND: Did he carve his eenitials on the palace
wall?

WALSH *takes her hand:* No, ELSKLING. On the
wall of fame. He's a pioneer—as much a pioneer
as the trail blazers who conquered our West,
fighting undaunted to their goal, while sceptics
jeered them. Barnum's like that. Crude? Perhaps.
. . . But his heart's as big as the world. Only America can appreciate a man like him. With us, he's
an institution.

LIND: Nevertheless, I weel not go to the banquet.

WALSH: Not even for me? If I promise he'll be-
have?

LIND *debates for a moment, then weakens:* It
seems I am always doing these eemposseeble things
for you. Yes. I go, but I warn you. . . .

WALSH: Thanks. We can't ruin P. T.,
ELSKLING. . . .   DISSOLVE TO:

---

197   INTERIOR: Banquet Hall in Hotel – Full Shot
      – Night

The guests are seated at a great horseshoe table. The
room is rich with American and Swedish flags. Barnum

has done himself proud. True to his word, Mr. Greeley is there, as well as the Mayor, Mr. Webster, Mr. Longfellow, the Astors, and many society women.

At the head of the table sits Jenny Lind. On one side of her is Barnum. On the other side is the Mayor. Next to Barnum sits Walsh.

There is a large string orchestra playing softly, from the mezzanine gallery.

CUT TO:

---

198   INTERIOR: Banquet Hall – Close Shot at Head of Table

Showing the lovely Jenny Lind talking with the Mayor. Walsh, on the opposite of Barnum, is talking with the Swedish Consul. Barnum is beaming, looking around the table. Suddenly he beckons off. The maître d'hôtel comes into the scene.

CUT TO:

---

199   INTERIOR: Banquet Hall – Closeup of Barnum and Maître d'Hôtel

---

The maître d'hôtel is leaning over Barnum's shoulder.
BARNUM *in stage whisper:* You fixed it with the band? They understand when I raise my right hand, they play the Swedish national anthem? *The maître d'hôtel nods.* And don't forgit! When I strike this gong ... *indicates gong attached to side*

168

of table ... that's the signal to bring in the cake!
MAÎTRE D'HÔTEL: ABSOLUMENT, MONSIEUR. ...
BARNUM: And the favors for the ladies?
MAÎTRE D'HÔTEL: They're being distributed now, Monsieur Barnum.
BARNUM: Good!

He looks about, smiles expectantly, then raises his right hand.

CUT TO:

---

200 INTERIOR: Banquet Hall—Flash of Orchestra in Gallery

As the maestro picks up Barnum's signal, nods to the musicians, and they barge into the Swedish national anthem.

CUT TO:

---

201 INTERIOR: Banquet Hall—Close Shot at Head of Table

The Swedish Consul gets to his feet, stands at military attention. Lind and Barnum are also on their feet. The Mayor looks slightly bewildered, but gets to his feet, as does Walsh.

CUT TO:

169

202 INTERIOR: Banquet Hall—High Crane Shot

Showing everyone rising and standing at attention. The waiters, however, are moving about, distributing the favors.

CUT TO:

203 CLOSEUP OF BARNUM—INTERIOR: Banquet Hall

He is feeling very pleased with himself, but enough is enough. He wigwags his hands, and the Swedish anthem comes to an abrupt halt.

BARNUM: Ladies and Gentlemen, be seated....

204 INTERIOR: Banquet Hall—Long Shot—Flash

As everyone, a little surprised, sits down.

CUT TO:

205 INTERIOR: Banquet Hall—Close Shot at Head of Table

Including Barnum, Lind and Walsh. Walsh is looking up at Barnum, who is still on his feet, with apprehension.

BARNUM: In the way of a little surprise, I've

presented all of the ladies favors....Be so good as to look at 'em.

Lind looks down at the fan beside her plate, a little surprised.

CUT TO:

---

206 INTERIOR: Banquet Hall—Close Shot at Group of Society Women (The Social Arbiters of the Bearded Lady Examination)

Curiously, they reach down to pick up the fans.

BARNUM'S VOICE: I don't mind tellin' you them tokens of my esteem cost me a lotta money....

CUT TO:

---

207 INTERIOR: Banquet Hall—Close Shot at Head of Table

Including Barnum, Walsh and Lind. Lind looks at Barnum incredulously. Walsh's collar begins to wilt.

BARNUM *continuing—grinning:* Each one of them cost me.... *Walsh gives Barnum's coattail a terrific jerk—he looks startled, and finishes.* ... Well, they cost plenty. You'll notice in the handle of 'em, there's a genuwine Mexican sapphire....

CUT TO:

208 INTERIOR: Banquet Hall—Close Shot at Group of Society Women

They are so dazed by Barnum's speech, that they are hypnotized into opening the fans.

CUT TO:

209 CLOSEUP OF FAN IN WOMAN'S HAND—INTERIOR: Banquet Hall

On one side of the fan is a picture of Jenny Lind, with the caption "THE GREATEST DIVA IN THE WORLD." The fan is turned over in the woman's hand and on the other side is a picture of Barnum with his midgets, and the slogan: "THE GREATEST IMPRESARIO IN THE WORLD."

CUT TO:

210 INTERIOR: Banquet Hall—Closeup of Two Society Women—Flash

They look at each other, stunned.
    FIRST WOMAN: It's incredible.
    SECOND WOMAN: I can't believe it.

CUT TO:

211   INTERIOR: Banquet Hall—Longer Shot

Showing Barnum grinning happily as he sees the women staring at the fans.

BARNUM *to the women:* Sorta cute idee, ain't it? *To a waiter:* Hey, monsewer George, there's a lady that didn't get one of them fans.... *He has raised his right hand to call the waiter.*

Immediately, on SOUND TRACK, the band blares out with the Swedish national anthem. The startled people, led by the Swedish Consul, get to their feet.

CUT TO:

212   INTERIOR: Banquet Hall—Close Shot of Barnum, Walsh and Swedish Consul

Standing at attention at head of table. The Swedish Consul is perspiring.

SWEDISH CONSUL *speaking out of side of his mouth to Walsh:* Is Mr. Barnum being funny, or insulting? As Swedish Consul, I resent any ...

WALSH *to the bewildered Barnum:* How do you turn it off?

Barnum, galvanized into action, wigwags again to the band. It stops abruptly. Walsh is tugging at Barnum's coat-tails.

WALSH: For Heaven's sake, sit down and STAY down.

They all sit down.

> BARNUM *like a child who has been slapped:*
> What've I done, Mr. Walsh? ... I paid twelve-
> fifty apiece for them fans.... CUT TO:

---

213 CLOSEUP OF JENNY LIND—INTERIOR: Banquet Hall

Her lips are compressed as she clutches the closed fan
in her hand, then slides it off with an angry whisk of
her hand to the floor. CUT TO:

---

214 INTERIOR: Banquet Hall—Quick Flashes of
People at the Table

Talking to one another.

> GREELEY *sarcastically:* A diamond in the rough.
> ASTOR: He's an impossible windbag.
> WOMAN: Let's slip out of here.
> DOWAGER *raising her lorgnette:* Merciful
> Heavens—look! CUT TO:

---

215 INTERIOR: Banquet Hall—Longer Shot

The waiters, dressed in fantastic costumes, come in
bearing the food. These colored gentry are feeling most
uncomfortable in white robes. CUT TO:

174

CLOSEUP OF WALSH AND BARNUM—INTE-
RIOR: Banquet Hall

Walsh is in a nightmare.

> WALSH *between clenched teeth—to Barnum:* Are
> you deliberately TRYING to make an ass of your-
> self?
>
> BARNUM *plaintively:* Nothin's too good for the
> little nightingale.
>
> WALSH *sighing:* Perhaps the Mayor can save
> the day. *His expression gets over that he doubts
> it, but he rises for order.* Ladies and Gentlemen,
> it is my great privilege and pleasure to introduce
> to you, his Honor, the Mayor. . . .

There is applause.

CUT TO:

---

217 INTERIOR: Banquet Hall—Longer Shot
Around Table

The Mayor starts to rise, but at this moment the irre-
pressible Barnum gets to his feet first.

> BARNUM: Jest a minute, please, Mr. Mayor,
> before you begin. . . . I got something . . . to. . . .
> *Unconsciously, he again raises his right hand.*

The band starts two bars of the Swedish national
anthem.

CUT TO:

Purple with rage, he mechanically gets to his feet.

CUT TO:

219   INTERIOR: Banquet Hall—Close Shot at End
of Table

Barnum furiously wigwags to the band, which breaks
off.

> BARNUM: Consarn it—I beg your pardon, La-
> dies and Gentlemen. . . . I jest wanted to say. . . .
> *The annoyed and discomfited Mayor sits down.*
> There's plenty a champagne—drink all you want.
> . . . I'm a teetotaller myself, but don't let that stop
> you. . . . This is Liberty Hall!

Walsh leaps into the breach, jumps to his feet and
raises his champagne glass.

> WALSH: A toast to our guest of honor—Madame
> Jenny Lind!

CUT TO:

220   INTERIOR: Banquet Hall—Full Shot of Table

Showing everyone rising, taking up glasses.

CUT TO:

Barnum and Walsh coming down the gangplank with Jenny Lind on her arrival in America.

221 CLOSEUP OF BARNUM AND WALSH – INTE-
RIOR: Banquet Hall

Walsh has his glass upraised, Barnum is bewildered.

    BARNUM *to Walsh:* What'll I say?

    WALSH *out of the side of his mouth:* Nothing!
... Drink!

    VOICES OF GUESTS *ad libbing—on* SOUND
TRACK: To Jenny Lind. ... Miss Lind. ...

Barnum is staring at his wine glass, hypnotized—then
with a do-or-die expression, he grabs the glass, starts
to drink. The first bubbles go up his nose, causing him
to make a wry face, but he manfully downs the contents
of the glass. Walsh stares at him in amazement just as
he finishes.

    BARNUM *a Christopher Columbus:* Tastes like
cider.

                         C U T   T O :

222 INTERIOR: Banquet Hall – Longer Shot

Everyone has started to sit down following the toast,
except Barnum, who remains on his feet.

                          C U T   T O :

223 INTERIOR: Banquet Hall – Close Shot at Head of Table

Including Barnum, Walsh, Lind, the Swedish Consul and Mayor. Barnum is still on his feet. He is pouring out another glass of champagne. Now he raises it triumphantly and looks at Lind.

BARNUM *at the top of his voice:* Now let me propose a toast to the lovely Swedish Nightingale. ... *He gives a world's record burp.* GESUNDHEIT!

CUT TO:

223A INTERIOR: Banquet Hall – Close Shot at Society Group Including Mr. Astor

They all look astounded. On SOUND TRACK is a second lusty burp.

CUT TO:

224 INTERIOR: Banquet Hall – Close Shot at Head of Table

Including Barnum, Walsh, Lind, the Swedish Consul and the Mayor. Barnum smiles amiably as though nothing had happened.

BARNUM *continuing:* ... You who ain't Swedish may not understand my toast, but SHE will.... *Takes a deep breath:* YAG MAR KIME KIN DU!

178

Lind's face goes scarlet, she is horror-stricken. The Consul is on the verge of apoplexy. Walsh gives a gasp.

LIND *horrified:* Meester Barnum!

WALSH: You fool! Do you know what you're saying?

CUT TO:

224A INTERIOR: Banquet Hall – Close Shot at Swedish Consul, Greeley and Two Other Men

---

The outraged Consul is leaning across the table, whispering in the ears of the other men, telling them the meaning of the phrase. They are outraged also.

BARNUM'S VOICE *on* SOUND TRACK: A course, I know what I'm sayin'. . . .

CUT TO:

---

225 INTERIOR: Banquet Hall – Close Shot at Society Group Including Mr. Astor

---

They are frozen with indignation. One woman, knowing something is wrong, turns to Mr. Astor.

WOMAN *to Mr. Astor:* What does it mean?

MR. ASTOR *virtuously:* Madame, I've never even said it in ENGLISH.

He pushes back his chair.

CUT TO:

226 INTERIOR: Banquet Hall – Close Shot at Head of Table

Barnum is still on his feet, slightly bewildered. Jenny Lind, outraged, is getting to her feet. Walsh is behind her.

> LIND *in tears—to Walsh:* Take me away!
> SWEDISH CONSUL *getting to his feet—indignantly:* An insult to my country . . . to my country-woman!
> BARNUM: But Ole taught me. . . . I ain't ashamed to say it, Jen—Madame Lind. . . . It's from my heart when I say, YAG MAR—
> WALSH *gives him a shake:* Shut up! You've ruined everything!

He takes the hysterical, humiliated Lind out.

> BARNUM *pathetically:* Mr. Walsh. . . .

The Mayor is standing. Walsh has left with Lind. The Swedish Consul is throwing down his napkin in fury. Barnum looks around, bewildered.

CUT TO:

227 INTERIOR: Banquet Hall – Longer Shot

People are getting to their feet, outraged, disgusted, starting to go.

CUT TO:

228   INTERIOR: Banquet Hall – Close Shot at Head of Table

Barnum, dazed and pathetic, is looking at the people passing him.

    BARNUM *to various ones passing him:* You ain't goin', Mr. Greeley? *Then to the Swedish Consul:* Why should she get mad? . . . I only said, "I think you are the loveliest woman in the world." . . . Ole told me.

    SWEDISH CONSUL *infuriated—not believing him:* DU JUGER! (Means—"You liar!") *He brushes past Barnum.*

    BARNUM *to the Mayor:* YOU ain't leavin', too, Mr. Mayor?

    MAYOR *coughing:* Sorry . . . Official business. . . . Good night.

                      C U T T O :

229   INTERIOR: Banquet Hall – Close Shot at Door Leading Outside

On hand, is the noisy Skiff, listening to the indignant people who brush past him. As Greeley passes, Skiff steps in front of him.

    GREELEY *to Skiff—his tone ominous for Barnum:* I want to talk with you! *Skiff's eyes bulge with excitement.*

                      C U T T O :

181

229A CLOSEUP BARNUM AT TABLE—INTERIOR:
Banquet Hall

Looking bewildered—piteous! The last man to leave is hurrying past the table when, in his haste, he over-turns a chair. There is the resounding sound of the gong (the signal for the cake)—Barnum is too bewildered to be conscious of the ringing gong.

CUT TO:

230 INTERIOR: Banquet Hall— Long Shot

Practically everyone has gone now. Barnum is look-ing after the departing guests. At this moment (from the signal of the gong) ten waiters in Court costume, knee breeches and powdered wigs, move majestically into the banquet hall, carrying either a huge cake with Jenny Lind's name on it, or nine small cakes, each with an initial spelling out her name. As Barnum sees them, he raises an imploring right hand, and—the SWEDISH NATIONAL ANTHEM BOOMS OUT.

CUT TO:

231 CLOSEUP OF BARNUM AT TABLE—INTERIOR:
Banquet Hall

This is the last straw. In desperation, he reaches for a full bottle of champagne, pours a waterglass full, and starts to down it, as the Swedish national anthem plays on.

DISSOLVE TO:

---

232   INTERIOR: Railroad Station—Close Shot of Nancy and Ellen— Night

---

Seated together on a bench, waiting. On SOUND TRACK we hear noises of a departing train. Nancy is erect on the edge of the seat. There is a fanatical quality to her stare, as though she were communing with higher powers. Ellen is slumped back, her eyes heavy-lidded.

NANCY *the inspiration arrives:* Ellen! I see it clear. We were MEANT to miss that train!

ELLEN *looks up, startled:* What? . . . Why?

NANCY: Hallelujah! A revelation. . . . *Pausing— quoting:* "For better or for worse—till death us do part." . . . *Gets to her feet.* Phineas Barnum needs me! *Ellen also stands up.* I'm goin' to him. . . . *Suddenly remembering something, she blanches:* Ellen! Go home as fast as you can. Bring me that letter I left for Phineas. *Seizes Ellen's shoulders fiercely.* He mustn't see it. Bring it to the hotel. I won't rest easy till I have it in my own hands again!

DISSOLVE TO:

183

233   INTERIOR: Banquet Hall – Long Shot – Night

Every guest has left; the band has departed. The waiters are finishing clearing the tables, looking with disgust at Barnum who is slumped over the table in foreground in a drunken stupor. Three empty champagne bottles are beside him on the table. Two waiters are clearing off the table beside Barnum.

> FIRST WAITER *to helper—indicating Barnum:* What'll we do with it?
> SECOND WAITER: Leave it lay.

At this moment, Nancy appears at the doorway in background.

CUT TO:

234   CLOSEUP OF NANCY IN DOORWAY – INTERIOR: Banquet Hall

Nancy is looking off at Barnum. In an instant she takes in the situation. She sways—it is too much for her. She turns as though to go back, then changes her mind. . . . She cannot leave him alone like this.

CUT TO:

235   INTERIOR: Banquet Hall – Long Shot

Barnum, in the foreground, is still unconscious with his head on the table. In the background, Nancy is walking slowly toward him. She has the air of moving up to have one last look before the coffin is closed.

DISSOLVE TO:

---

236   INTERIOR: Hotel Bedroom—Close Shot at Bed—Late Night

Barnum is draped on the bed, mouth ajar, wheezing like a punctured bellows. Nancy is standing alongside the bed. Two waiters are just leaving the room.

NANCY *in dead voice—to waiters:* Thanks for carryin' him up.

Nancy stands, immobile, staring at the bed as though Barnum were a stranger. There is a knock on the door, and Ellen enters, breathless. She is holding the letter.

ELLEN *holding the letter:* They told me. . . . *Sees her defunct Uncle Phineas.* What's the matter?

Nancy appears to see Ellen for the first time. Without speaking, she holds out her hand for the letter. Ellen timidly gives it to her.

NANCY *in a dull, dead voice:* Wait for me outside. . . .

Ellen, fearful, backs across to the door which closes behind her. Nancy looks down at Barnum—her lips move.

NANCY *continuing:* "Till death us do part." . . . The man I married—is dead.

She pulls the sheet about his shoulders, then places the

185

letter in plain sight on the bureau, turns and walks out of the room, closing the door behind her.

DISSOLVE TO:

---

237 CLOSEUP NEWSPAPER INSERT: Day, Morning

The newspaper, Mr. Greeley's *Globe,* is on a bed. An article signed by Skiff narrating the atrocities of the previous evening leads the first-page news. The paper is dated 1840.

It reads:

"JENNY LIND IN TEARS
AS BARNUM DISGRACES
SELF AT BIG BANQUET

"Giddy Phineas T. Barnum, outdoing even HIS own customary eccentricities, last night startled and shocked a group of one hundred social and civic leaders of this community. Bawling like a calf, he sent his singer, Miss Jenny Lind, into hysteria as he made himself obnoxious to all concerned. The scene of the disgraceful episode was the Irving Hotel grand ball room."

Barnum's voice comes over SOUND TRACK.

BARNUM'S VOICE: What of I done to deserve this?

CAMERA PANS UP to pick up—

238　INTERIOR: Barnum's Hotel Bedroom—Close
Shot of Barnum—Morning

Sitting in bed in the hotel room, a jaded, dispirited
mortal, massaging his temples with a chunk of ice. A
large pitcher of ice water is beside the bed. Barnum,
dressed only in his long underwear, starts out of bed.

> BARNUM: It's a lie! *As he hits the floor, he
> lurches and grabs hold of his head. He calls out
> like a bewildered child:* Nancy...! *He looks
> about the strange room, obviously not knowing
> just where he is. Startled, almost frightened, he
> calls again:* Nan-cee!

He starts for the door to the hall, throws it open, then
stands there, amazed.

CUT TO:

239　INTERIOR: Barnum's Hotel Bedroom—Closeup Barnum

Propped in the doorway leading to the hall, his back to
the CAMERA. Through the hall a steady stream of porters and bellboys are pushing luggage-barrows upon
which are piled trunks and bags.

CUT TO:

187

240   INTERIOR: Barnum's Hotel Bedroom – Reverse Angle – Closeup of Barnum

As he stares, pop-eyed, and sees—
               C U T   T O :

241   INTERIOR: Hotel Hallway – Outside Barnum's Bedroom – Close Shot at Trunks on Passing Truck

Showing the luggage on which is painted in large letters:

             "MME. LIND"
               C U T   T O :

242   INTERIOR: Hotel Corridor – Closeup Barnum in Doorway Leading to Bedroom

His head wags and bobbles in visual synchronization with each passing truck. He gets dizzier and dizzier.
      BARNUM *at sea on a raft:* What IS this? Where AM I?
               C U T   T O :

243   INTERIOR: Hotel Corridor – Shooting Across Passing Trucks to Barnum

Weaving in the doorway. The trucks are passing before him.

BARNUM *continuing—to porter:* Where you takin' Madamwaselle Lind's satchels?

PORTER: To the boat, sir. . . . She's sailing today.

BARNUM: Sailin'! You're crazy!

CUT TO:

---

244 INTERIOR: Barnum's Hotel Room—Medium Shot

As Barnum turns from the open doorway.

BARNUM: She can't do that. . . . *He cavorts helplessly.* Where's Mr. Walsh?

His eyes light on his Inverness cape hanging over a chair. He seizes it, puts it on over his underwear and gallops out of the room.

CUT TO:

---

245 INTERIOR: Hotel Corridor—Showing Open Doors to Lind's Suite in Foreground

---

Barnum, a flying jaguar, the Inverness cape draped about him, his feet naked, charges to the door of Lind's apartment just as another porter comes out with luggage. Barnum suddenly realizes where he is. He stops short, looks befuddled, starts into the room.

CUT TO:

246 CLOSEUP OF BARNUM—REVERSE SHOT: Shooting from Lind's Apartment toward Hall Doorway

As Barnum lurches groggily into the room. He again stops, dazed. His eyes strain.

CUT TO:

247 INTERIOR: Living Room of Jenny Lind's Hotel Suite—Close Shot of Walsh and Lind—from Barnum's Angle

Lind and Walsh are standing near the piano. Walsh is just settling Lind's fur dolman about her shoulders. She is looking up, smiling and adoring him. He gazes on her tenderly.

LIND: MIN ELSKLING, this has all been a horreeble nightmare—but today starts for us a beautiful dream.

She pats his cheek.

CUT TO:

248 INTERIOR: Jenny Lind's Hotel Living Room —Closeup Barnum at Door

His eyes are toy balloons.

BARNUM *hoarse as a file:* Jenny!

CUT TO:

249 INTERIOR: Jenny Lind's Living Room— Hotel Apartment—Long Shot

Barnum can't believe his eyes. Lind and Walsh turn, startled.

BARNUM: So! Traitors! *He lurches in—his voice breaks:* Jenny, you can't do this to me. You CAN'T...

WALSH *calmly:* Go easy, Barnum.

He starts toward Barnum, over his shoulder giving Lind a look which indicates she wait in the next room. She hesitates.

BARNUM *through his teeth—to Walsh:* You took her from behind my back! You snake!

WALSH: Just a minute, P. T.... Don't blame me for your own stupidity.

BARNUM *bellowing:* Stupid! You call me...

WALSH: Putting it mildly.

BARNUM *leaping toward him:* You painted sepulchre!

Barnum leaps on Walsh, and Walsh, unprepared for the onslaught, goes down with Barnum on top. Barnum has a death grip on Walsh's throat and is strangling him. He is berserk, as he mutters—

BARNUM: Stab me in the back, will yuh?

He is shaking Walsh like a terrier shakes a rat. Lind screams.

LIND: Let heem alone! You—you fool! HELP!

191

He's keeling MIN ELSKLING! *She rushes to the door—yells down the hall:* Help!

The hotel force—the porters and bellboys who were carrying out Lind's luggage—come galloping into the room.

CUT TO:

---

250   INTERIOR: Jenny Lind's Hotel Living Room
       —Another Angle

Barnum is shaking Walsh like one gone mad. He has his thumbs on Walsh's windpipe. Walsh is almost done in. The bellboys and porters try to pull Barnum off.

LIND: Help! He weel keel heem!

Into this scene, strides the house detective—a broad-booted burley—revolver in his hand.

HOUSE DETECTIVE *to Barnum:* Git up! Or I'll run ye in! This is a respectable hotel.

He puts his revolver in his pocket, and joins in pulling the struggling Barnum off Walsh's chest. It takes four men to accomplish this little stint.

CUT TO:

---

251   INTERIOR: Jenny Lind's Hotel Living Room
       —(Shooting from Corridor into Room)

The house detective and three porters are dragging **Barnum** from the room.

Barnum (Beery) welcomes Jenny Lind (Virginia Bruce) to America.

BARNUM *telling the world:* I'll kill him! He'll never bunko another trustin' friend!

They take the struggling Barnum out of the room, down the corridor, past CAMERA. In the room, in background, Walsh is just starting to sit up. He is clutching his throat. Lind throws herself to her knees beside him, and puts her arms around him.

CUT TO:

---

252 INTERIOR: Barnum's Hotel Bedroom—Medium Shot

The house detective and the bellboys are depositing the still threshing Barnum in his room. Barnum has his arms about the house detective's beltline, but the officer throws him off. We get a flash of Barnum's swift and sly movement as he takes something from the detective's pocket.

HOUSE DETECTIVE *panting:* Now you stay put!

He slams the door on Barnum and we hear the lock being turned from outside. Barnum has a cunning expression as he reveals the gun which he has taken from the house detective. He is ready to kill Walsh. He tries the door—it is locked. But there is a transom, and he surveys it as though planning to try an escape there. He drags the heavy bureau to the door, and is about to climb up when he sees the letter which Nancy has left, addressed to him. A curious, puzzled look comes to his face. He postpones his climb to tear open the envelope. He starts to read.

He seems like a man stricken—he cannot comprehend fully. The gun drops to the floor unheeded. Even when the door is unlocked and the house detective forces open the door, pushing back the bureau far enough to allow him to enter, Barnum does not notice. His eyes are frozen on the letter.

> HOUSE DETECTIVE: Pretty smart, ain't cha? Now just gimme back that gun.

He sees the gun and picks it up, greatly relieved. Barnum looks at the intruder, his face tragic.

> BARNUM *as though speaking to himself:* She says she's goin' back to where she belongs—

He crumples the letter and looks into space.

> HOUSE DETECTIVE: Bad news, Mr. Barnum? You ain't sick?

Barnum attempts to cover up.

> BARNUM: No . . . jest somethin' I et. . . .

FADE OUT:

FADE IN:

---

253 EXTERIOR: Battery Park in New York— Night

Possibly a GLASS SHOT EFFECT showing the water and boats. The tooting of boat whistles punctuates the stillness of the night. There are silhouetted figures on several of the benches which line the paths. Tall, oil-lighted lamps cast feeble rays over the benches.

DISSOLVE TO:

254 EXTERIOR: Battery Park—Close Shot at Bench

SHOOTING with LOW CAMERA. INSERT shows the legs of a shabby bench-sitter. The shoes are worn, the trousers frayed and baggy. Coming toward CAMERA is the still jaunty General Tom Thumb, taking a small poodle dog for an airing. As the poochie comes alongside the derelict legs, he sniffs, and is about to hoist a haunch.

TOM THUMB *yanks the dog away:* Ain't you ashamed, Spud?

BARNUM'S VOICE *on* SOUND TRACK: Why should he be? You can't expect more from a dog than you can from humans.

As Barnum is speaking, the CAMERA PULLS BACK AND PANS UP to disclose—

255 EXTERIOR: Battery Park—Close Shot of Barnum, Tom Thumb and Dog

Barnum is seated on the bench, whittling aimlessly on a sprig. A tattered newspaper is on the bench beside him. The scene is illuminated by the oil lamp over his

195

head. Barnum has become resigned to fate. He grins rather sheepishly at Tom Thumb.

TOM THUMB: Why, Mr. Barnum!

BARNUM *trying to be sprightly:* Still prosperin', General?

TOM THUMB: We was mentioning your name only last night ... wonderin' what become of yuh....

BARNUM *carelessly:* Oh, I been around.... Lotsa big business deals comin' up.... *Tom listens respectfully. Barnum stretches:* A course, the last year or so, been spendin' lotsa time at the Hot Springs ... little touch a rheumatism....

TOM THUMB: Too bad, Mr. Barnum.... *Then casually:* Just on my way home to supper.... Won't you come along?

Barnum's mouth waters at the thought of food, but he masters himself.

BARNUM: Just et—thanks all the same....

TOM THUMB *urging him:* Lavinia'd like to see yuh.

BARNUM *reminiscently:* Lavinia.... So you're still married, huh? 'Member how I used to hold her in the palm of my hand? *His eyes glow:* Just like a little doll....

DISSOLVE THROUGH TO:

196

256 INTERIOR: Tom Thumb's Flat—Night—
Closeup of Barnum

Holding Lavinia in his hand. Barnum has succumbed
to Tom Thumb's invitation, and is at his house. He is
grinning as he holds the little lady.

BARNUM: You ain't grown a mite, honey.

CUT TO:

257 INTERIOR: Tom Thumb's Living Room—
Long Shot

Barnum is standing in the center of the living room of
this unpretentious little flat, holding Lavinia in his
hand. The outstanding characteristic of this place is its
MINIATURE furniture. Barnum looms like Gulliver
among the Lilliputians in this doll-like environment.

LAVINIA: Seems like old times.

TOM THUMB *indicating the settee:* This may
fit you, Mr. Barnum.

BARNUM *puts Lavinia down and negotiates the
settee, which he fills to overflowing—to Lavinia:*
'Member, Lavinia, the time I was ballyhooin' yuh,
and the sacred monkey of Madagascar got loose
an' chawed me in the hips?

TOM THUMB *as Lavinia giggles reminiscently:*
That sure was presence of mind, Mr. Barnum, not

197

droppin' Lavinia.

LAVINIA *starting for the door:* If you'll excuse me a minute. . . . *She leaves the room.*

BARNUM: It's kinda like a dream. . . . *Reaching for his hat:* Well, I got to be runnin' along now. . . .

TOM THUMB: I was passin' the old Museum yestiddy—sure looked strange, standin' there so empty. . . .

Barnum's face twitches and he rises. It is not an easy task, for the settee clings to his hips.

TOM THUMB *continuing:* Looks like you'll HAVE to stay for dinner.

BARNUM *wrestling the settee loose:* Consarn it!

TOM THUMB: You still own the lease on the Museum, don'tcha?

BARNUM *free at last, puts the settee down:* Hum-m-m! I own lotsa things—on PAPER. *He puts out his hand:* Well, General, sure was good. . . .

TOM THUMB *takes his hand:* Why don't you open up again?

BARNUM: What with? Two years has gone over the dam, leavin' me no attractions, no wife . . . no nothin'. . . .

TOM THUMB: Didn't you try to get Mrs. Barnum back?

BARNUM: I'll not bore yah with the sad details.

TOM THUMB: You gotta pull yourself together, Mr. Barnum. . . .

Lavinia pokes her head through the door.

LAVINIA: Dinner's ready....

BARNUM: Good-bye, Lavinia....*He sniffs:* Hmmmmm. Smells like...

TOM THUMB: That's just what it is. A New England boiled dinner.

BARNUM *with a graveyard laugh:* Haa-a-a. Ain't had one o' them things since Nancy...*He gulps and turns his back, coughing to cover up:* That woman was wuth her weight in gold, General!

TOM THUMB: That she was, Mr. Barnum.... Step in here.... I gotta little surprise...

Barnum cannot hold out any longer. He turns to the door leading to the dining-room.

CUT TO:

---

258 INTERIOR: Tom Thumb's Flat – Closeup of Barnum Standing at Dining-Room Door

---

As he starts into room, he pauses, his eyes protruding.

BARNUM: Jumpin' Jehosophat!

CUT TO:

---

259 INTERIOR: Tom Thumb's Dining-Room – from Barnum's Angle

The furniture here, also, is of doll-house scale, although there are a few large chairs about the table. A long

199

table is set for dinner, in the midst of which is a New England boiled dinner in a great tureen. Standing about the table, all expectant and smiling, are the freaks—the Fat Woman, Tattooed Man, the Cardiff Giant, etc.

FREAKS *ad lib—in a chorus:* Hello, Mr. Barnum! Glad to see you. How are you, Mr. Barnum?

CUT TO:

---

260 CLOSEUP OF BARNUM—INTERIOR: Tom Thumb's Dining-Room

Dazed, Barnum starts to blubber.

BARNUM: Friends... jest seein' yuh all again ... none a yuh holdin' any mallets agin me....

VOICE *on* SOUND TRACK: Mr. Barnum....

His head snaps back like an irate charger's, as he looks off and sees—

CUT TO:

---

261 CLOSEUP BEARDED LADY—INTERIOR: Tom Thumb's Dining-Room

Standing in the doorway leading from the kitchen is the Bearded Lady. She is holding a coffee pot, and has an apron tied about her waist. She looks at Barnum pleadingly.

ZORRO: I was gonna keep hid in the kitchen, but when I heard your dear voice...

CUT TO:

INTERIOR: Tom Thumb's Dining-room—
Longer Shot

Barnum's eyes narrow, then he turns to Tom Thumb.

BARNUM *stiffly:* Sorry, I can't stay to supper.

TOM THUMB: Madame Zorro's repented.

ZORRO: Look at the gray hairs in my beard—
just from remorse....*She gulps:* It was the
money tempted me, Mr. Barnum....Yuh see, I
was gonna have a baby....

BARNUM: Illegiterate? My! My!

ZORRO: No. I lied to you when I posed as single
...but I paid for that falsehood. The twins ex-
pired.

BARNUM *forgives all:* The Lord taketh and the
Lord giveth away....I always knew you was a
lady.

He steps over to her to press her hand, but she throws
her arms about him. The coffee pot is dangling over his
shoulder. He pats her, barely avoiding the beard. A
stream of coffee runs from the spout, hits the middle of
Barnum's back. He leaps from her embrace.

BARNUM: Jumpin' Jehosophat!

Everyone hops to his aid—Lavinia, the Bearded Lady,
the Cardiff Giant, etc.

CUT TO:

263 CLOSEUP TOM THUMB—INTERIOR: Tom Thumb's Dining-Room

He is looking seriously at Barnum.

TOM THUMB: It was Fate steered us into each other tonight, Mr. Barnum....

CUT TO:

264 INTERIOR: Tom Thumb's Dining-Room— Longer Shot

The Bearded Lady holds Barnum's coat in her hand, wiping off the coffee stains. Barnum is in his shirt sleeves.

TOM THUMB *continuing:* ...twenty-four hours more, and it woulda been too late. We'd of all been signed up....

BARNUM *spirit returning:* Signed up with who?

TOM THUMB: None of us wanted to, but what could we do? We HAD to eat.

BARNUM: Who's opened a Museum? Who?

TOM THUMB: Mr. Skiff on Canal Street.

BARNUM *exploding:* Skiff! Thinks he can run a Museum, eh, what?

TOM THUMB: HE can't, Mr. Barnum, but YOU can. We'll work for you for nothin', till business gets going.

CUT TO:

265 CLOSEUP OF BARNUM AND TOM THUMB—
INTERIOR: Tom Thumb's Dining-Room

For a moment Barnum stands stunned by the offer.
VOICES OF FREAKS *including Bearded Lady's:*
You bet we will! Sure will, Mr. Barnum. Happiest
day of my life.
BARNUM *swallowing hard—looks down at Tom
Thumb:* General, you're the littlest man in the
world, but you're still a bigger man than I could
ever be!

DISSOLVE TO:

266 EXTERIOR: Alleyway Back of Barnum's
American Museum— Night

A huge truck is backed up to an open door, through
which can be seen a suggestion of the Museum. It is
the night before the re-opening of the Museum. The
lions in cages on the truck are roaring. Inside the
establishment can be seen workmen putting finishing
touches to the place, sounds of hammering, etc. Several
men are unloading crates of lions and tigers. All the
cages are on wheels. Tom Thumb is superintending the
delivery of the animals.
TOM THUMB *yelling into Museum:* Mr. Barnum, where do yuh want these cats put?

Barnum appears in the doorway in shirt sleeves. He is puffing, perspiring, and carries a hammer in his hand.

BARNUM *the czar again:* Put them critters right inside the door! *To Tom:* C'mon, General—got a job fur you.

Barnum darts back into the Museum, followed by Tom Thumb.

C U T   T O :

---

267 INTERIOR: Barnum's American Museum— Long Shot

Showing workmen putting up signs ... the incessant sound of hammering and shouting. Zebras and horses are being led across the background. Barnum strides in with the hammer in his hand, Tom Thumb running behind him.

C U T   T O :

---

268 INTERIOR: Barnum's American Museum— Follow Shot of Barnum and Tom Thumb

---

Barnum strides through, Tom Thumb trailing in background. Barnum calls to a carpenter.

BARNUM: Get a fancier sign for the Bearded Lady—make the spinach two feet longer! *He pantomimes.*

CARPENTER'S VOICE *from other side:* Is the

204

sign on the front entrance big enough, Mr. Barnum?

BARNUM: Haven't seen it, but make it twice as big. *He is prancing along.*

The Bearded Lady, wearing a man's short coat over her dress, strides across the scene with a ladder on her back. She carries a pail and brushes.

ZORRO *to Barnum:* Oughta see my platform, Mr. Barnum . . . I painted it baby blue and pink.

BARNUM: Will it be dry for tomorrow's opening?

ZORRO: I'm going to fan it dry.

As she starts to exit from the scene, Tod comes bustling in.

TOD: How about putting a coupla watchmen on the doors? I wouldn't trust that fellow Skiff as far as I could sling a dead cat.

BARNUM: I reckon he's plenty het up, all right. . . . *Bellowing off:* Hey, Mike! . . . Joe! *To Tod— in dismissal:* Attended to.

As Tod starts out, a couple of gnarled bruisers come into scene.

BARNUM: Lissen! We're working all night. You boys know everybody who belongs here?

They both nod.

BARNUM: Well, post yourselves at the doors, and if any stranger tries to get past, let him have a bunch of fives. *He expresses this clearly by doubling up his fist and executing a jab.* Understand?

205

MIKE *one of the bruisers:* Poifectly....

As the two start out, Barnum gives an exhausted "Whew!" and sits down heavily on a crate of monkeys. He is all in, breathing heavily, resting his chin in his hands. Tom Thumb picks up an antique placard from the floor and starts to fan him. It is an old Jenny Lind poster. Tom catches sight of it, realizes what it is, and turns it over hastily before Barnum can catch sight of it.

> BARNUM *the relaxed potentate:* Smell that saw-dust, General? As sweet as a bride. And me going in for the Arts.... *He laughs derisively—then turns, indicating Museum:* THIS is all I know— This is my life—the American public loves to be humbugged ... and I'm the PRINCE of Humbugs!
>
> CUT TO:

---

269   EXTERIOR: Barnum's American Museum— (Shooting from Opposite Side of Street)— Night

---

In foreground are two shadowy figures gazing at the lighted Museum across the street. Several workmen are putting up the sign:

> "GRAND OPENING TOMORROW"
>
> CUT TO:

206

270　EXTERIOR: Barnum's American Museum—
Closeup of Two Men in Shadows

They are standing across the street from the Museum.
One of the men is Skiff, the other his henchman.

> HENCHMAN: Rotten trick, guv'nor—him takin'
> them attractions right out from under your
> nose. . . .
>
> SKIFF *laughs nastily:* So he's goin' to open to-
> morrow, is he? Like hell he is. . . .

The henchman gets the note in Skiff's voice and turns
to him eagerly. Then both men start at something they
see across the street. On SOUND TRACK we hear the
noise of horses' hoofs clattering on cobblestones. The
two men shrink back in the shadows.

CUT TO:

271　EXTERIOR: Barnum's American Museum—
Medium Shot

An open carriage is just pulling up before the Museum.
We hear a rousing yodel and out of the cab steps none
other than Mr. Walsh. He is slightly inebriated, but
still his dandified, prosperous self. Several large bags
are piled up in the carriage, suggesting Mr. Walsh has
just returned from a long journey. He pulls out some
money, hands it to the driver with a flourish.

WALSH: Here, my good nuncle, take my worldly goods to the Astor House and reserve a royal suite.

Walsh advances upon the Museum with a jaunty air.

---

272   EXTERIOR: Barnum's American Museum—Close Shot at Front Door

---

Just as Walsh starts through the half open door of the Museum, two stalwart figures step out and confront him belligerently.

MIKE *one of the bruisers:* Where do yuh t'ink you're goin', cull?

WALSH: Inside.... Gentlemen.

JOE *the other bruiser:* De Museum opens tomorro' at noon!

He advances upon Walsh menacingly.

WALSH: Ah, but I can't wait until tomorrow.... You see I'm an old schoolmate of Mr. Barnum's, and....

MIKE: I imagine he'll live till tomorrer if he don't see you.... Now get goin'!

WALSH: Just as you say, my rude sirs—I can take a hint. *He raises his hat.* Pleasant dreams....

He starts down the street, swinging his cane, leaving the two men glaring.

CUT TO:

Banquet to Jenny Lind, Mr. Barnum spouting.

INTERIOR: Barnum's American Museum—
Medium Shot

Barnum is sitting on the monkey crate, his head thrown back—he has fallen asleep and is snoring. Tom Thumb comes in with Lavinia. They are carrying Barnum's supper tray between them, and place it on a box before him. He awakens.

> BARNUM *looking up wearily:* Mighty nice of you, Lavinia, fetching it all the way from the resterant, but I'm too plumb tuckered out to eat....

Lavinia whisks off the napkin which covers the tray. Barnum looks at it suspiciously.

> BARNUM: A New England boiled dinner?... There's only one woman could do justice by that masterpiece, and she's...*He gives a ponderous sigh—shakes his head.* If you don't mind...
> LAVINIA: Just taste it...
> BARNUM: Well, after all your trouble...*He tastes it gingerly—his expression changes—he takes another large gulp.* Jumpin' Jehosophat.... *Wonder in his tone.* It's a sacrilege to say so, but it tastes exactly like Nancy's!

The two midgets exchange glances.

> NANCY'S VOICE (on SOUND TRACK): Well, it oughta, Phineas Barnum....

Barnum gasps, looks off. The midgets smile at each other.

CUT TO:

---

274   INTERIOR: Barnum's American Museum—Close Shot of Nancy (with Ellen in Background)

Nancy, much the same as we saw her in earlier scenes, stands before him, wearing a hat and dolman. Behind her is Ellen, prettier than ever, a far-away look in her eyes.

    NANCY *continuing:* ... seein' as how I cooked it. When Tom and Lavinia wrote and told me the kinda truck you was puttin' in your stummick, I thought I better come and save your life....

CUT TO:

---

275   INTERIOR: Barnum's American Museum—Longer Shot

To include Barnum, Nancy, Ellen and the midgets. Barnum is still gaping.

    BARNUM *gasping like a geyser:* Nancy! ...

    NANCY *surveys the scene:* Openin' up again, eh? Never profit by experience, do you, Phineas?

Barnum gets to his feet.

    BARNUM: Nancy! ... Sweetheart! *He starts toward her.*

CUT TO:

276 CLOSEUP OF BARNUM AND NANCY — IN-TERIOR: Barnum's American Museum

Nancy is stiff and uncompromising, as Barnum stumbles toward her.

> BARNUM *choking:* You're GONNA stay with me, aren't you?
>
> NANCY: Papa said I was a spineless, unprincipled, weak sister....
>
> BARNUM: Blast Papa!
>
> NANCY *with a gulp:* That's what I said.... *Buries her head on his bosom:* Phineas!...

His arms go about her, and he holds her tenderly, on the verge of tears himself. CUT TO:

277 CLOSE SHOT OF TOM THUMB, LAVINIA AND ELLEN

The two midgets and Ellen look on in silence. Their eyes are dim too. Tom presses his wife's hand. She snuggles close to him.

278 INTERIOR: Barnum's American Museum — Medium Shot of Group

Nancy is the first to pull herself together.

> NANCY: Your vittels is gettin' cold, Phineas.

He sits down on the crate, wipes away his tears, blows his nose with a terrific roar. Nancy starts to feed him.

CUT TO:

279 INTERIOR: Barnum's American Museum— Close Shot at Back Door (Shooting into Alleyway)

Mike comes into scene from CAMERA, starting toward the open door leading to the alleyway.

MIKE *calling back over his shoulder:* You stay on the front—I'll watch de alley.

CUT TO:

280 EXTERIOR: Alleyway in Rear of Museum (Showing Door Leading into Museum)

In the lighted doorway stands the truculent Mike, while in the shadows of the rear Museum wall comes Walsh, en route to the back door. He pauses as he hears Mike's speech.

MIKE *bellowing back:* And if any more strange dudes show up . . .

CUT TO:

281 CLOSEUP OF WALSH

Standing in the shadows of the rear wall. Mike's voice comes over SOUND TRACK—

MIKE'S VOICE *continuing from last scene:* ...
give it to 'em first and ast 'em questions after!
For a moment Mr. Walsh is in a quandary. Then another voice is heard—that of a drayman.

DRAYMAN'S VOICE *from other direction— over* SOUND TRACK: Gimme a hand—we gotta git all these crates inside!

A sudden light dawns on Walsh—an inspiration! He grins, and eases out in the direction of this last voice.

CUT TO:

---

282   INTERIOR: Barnum's American Museum—Medium Shot of Group

---

Barnum is eating—the contented bull chewing his cud. He talks with his mouth full, addressing Ellen.

BARNUM: Did you get married yet, honey?

NANCY *answering for her ward:* She's had lots o' good, respectable prospects, but she's still got that FRIEND o' yours on her mind ... *Scathingly:* ... that friend o' yours with the three million precious brain cells. ...

BARNUM: Just another mistake, Nancy ... If he ever had three million brain cells, they all blew out at once. What's more, he ain't any friend. ... He knows better'n come near me—that's why he's been hiding in Yurrup. I don't never want to HEAR his NAME again!

CUT TO:

213

Showing two men unloading boxes in the shadows.
Walsh is standing on the opposite side of the dray, so
that the dray wagon is between him and the watchful
Mike, and is holding up two bills to one of the unload-
ers, urging the man to accept.

WALSH: Twenty dollars ... ten dollars apiece
... Just a joke on my old friend P. T. *Indicates
an Egyptian mummy case on the ground:* All you
have to do is carry me in and set me down in front
of him.

The other man has been casting avid eyes on the two
ten-dollar bills.

FIRST UNLOADER: Twenty dollars is a lot of
money.

SECOND UNLOADER: *Taking the currency:*
And it's a long way to pay day.... *To Walsh—
with the air of one placating a lunatic:* Hop in,
feller.

Walsh grins. The man opens up the lid of the mummy
case and Walsh gets inside. The men close the lid and
pick up the coffin.

CUT TO:

284 EXTERIOR: Barnum's American Museum—
Close Shot at Back Entrance

Mike, who is standing on guard, straightens up alertly as the two draymen come staggering through under the weight of the Egyptian mummy case. Mike gives them the office, with his thumb, to pass inside.

CUT TO:

285 INTERIOR: Barnum's American Museum—
Another Angle

Showing workmen bustling about; other draymen unloading their cargo. The two conspirators with their Egyptian mummy case are headed toward Barnum, who is in the background, still eating his dinner. Just as the two men pass the foot of the steps, Tod comes dashing in.

TOD *to the draymen:* Here, drop that thing! *As they start guiltily:* Give the boys a hand with the lion cage!
FIRST DRAYMAN: But we gotta—
TOD *grabbing the man by the arm:* C'mon! Do you want those cats to get loose? *To the other yeoman:* Come along!
The two conspirators put down the mummy case, and Tod hastens them out of scene. They keep looking back

anxiously, and just as they leave the scene, Sam, the erstwhile painter who is acting as foreman, comes in with four men who are carrying a huge barrel. As they start toward the stairs with it, Sam sees the mummy case and frowns.

SAM *giving orders:* Here—one of you fellows— gimme a lift with this.... *Indicates the mummy case:* ... goes up on the balcony.

The men with the barrel put their burden down, and one of the crew helps Sam lift the mummy case. They start up the stairs. The remaining three men strain to lift the barrel again and follow up the stairs.

---

286   CLOSEUP OF WALSH — Inside the Case

He is wondering what is happening; he starts to open the lid, then decides to wait a while.

---

287   INTERIOR: Barnum's American Museum — Medium Shot of Upper Balcony on Second Floor

---

The balcony is littered with unpacked boxes and crates. Sam and his helper stagger in with the mummy case, drop it on the floor, and as they straighten up, the other three men come in with the barrel.

SAM *indicating the mummy case:* Put it down on there till we find a place....

The men deposit the heavy barrel on top of the Egyptian mummy case, in which reposes poor Mr. Walsh, and start out of scene, their minds on other business.

CUT TO:

288 INTERIOR: Barnum's American Museum—Close Shot of Mummy Case (Showing Barrel on Top)

Mr. Walsh is making a feeble effort to open the lid from the inside. It gives about an inch. Walsh kicks on the mummy case, and starts to yell.

WALSH'S VOICE: Help! Let me out! Help!
His voice is muffled. The lid clamps shut again.

CUT TO:

289 INTERIOR: Barnum's American Museum—Close Shot of Group

Barnum has finished eating. He wipes his mouth with the back of his hand, smiles fondly at Nancy and Ellen. Then, with great decision, he gets to his feet, yanks up his trousers.

BARNUM: Just make yourselves at home, folks. ...Lotta work to be done before tomorrow.... *To Tom Thumb:* General, get some of the boys to help me unpack those boxes upstairs.

As Tom Thumb goes out of scene, Barnum sniffs the air suspiciously:

BARNUM: Do I smell smoke?

CUT TO:

290   EXTERIOR: Barnum's American Museum— Medium Shot in Alleyway

Showing a small conflagration in back of the building, flames shooting up the wall and through a window. (NOTE: Two or three QUICK FLASHES, showing various parts of the building burning, getting over the idea that Skiff has set fire to the structure in several places.) Into one of these scenes runs the valiant Mike.

MIKE *bawling out:* Mr. Barnum!

291   INTERIOR: Barnum's American Museum— (Shooting toward Back Wall)

Showing the flames streaking up past window, on the outside.

VOICES *on* SOUND TRACK: The place is afire! ... Git the water buckets! ... Mr. Barnum! What'll we do?

CUT TO:

292 INTERIOR: Barnum's American Museum— Close Shot of Group

Barnum leaps into action, wildly excited. Nancy, Lavinia and Ellen are struck speechless.

    BARNUM *almost hysterical:* Compose yourselves, and turn in the alarm! Bring out the hose! *To the women:* You women get outside!

CUT TO:

293 EXTERIOR: Barnum's American Museum— Longer Shot

Showing smoke billowing through windows.
On SOUND TRACK, the tumult of gathering crowds, shouts and shattering glass.

CUT TO:

294 INTERIOR: Barnum's American Museum— Longer Shot—Flash

Showing fire progressing—more smoke than flames. Workmen have turned firemen, throwing pails of water —an ineffectual effort. Banners are burning, lithographs peeling and cooking. On SOUND TRACK we hear the roar and screaming of trapped animals.

CUT TO:

219

295   INTERIOR: Barnum's American Museum—
Flash—Near Tom Thumb's Platform

Showing Tom Thumb carrying Lavinia out of the inferno. She has fainted. Tom stumbles with his burden
and falls. On SOUND TRACK the cries of animals are
intensified.

296   INTERIOR: Barnum's American Museum—
Close Shot at Menagerie

Showing the cages on wheels filled with lions and tigers,
smoke rising in weaving pillars about their dens. The
animals are charging against the bars, roaring and
howling. Attendants are hurling buckets of water on
hay, straw and the cages.

CUT TO:

297   EXTERIOR: Barnum's American Museum—
Close Shot toward Rear Entrance (Shooting
from Alleyway)

Barnum, singed and tattered, comes through the blaze
and smoke, carrying Tom and Lavinia, unconscious,
under either arm. Nancy and Ellen follow—they all
run out of danger to the street. The fire is burning
much more briskly at back of Museum, but the rest

220

of the building is filled with smoke.

> BARNUM *inviting the world in general:* Come on, everybody! Help those pore animals out!

Barnum runs back into the Museum, followed by some of the crowd.

CUT TO:

---

298   EXTERIOR: Street Near Barnum's American Museum

The hose carts, drawn by men, come clanging and swaying down the street, the bells ringing fiercely.

CUT TO:

---

299   INTERIOR: Barnum's American Museum— Close Shot of Balcony on Second Floor

---

Showing the Egyptian mummy case in a conspicuous place. Smoke is beginning to drift up, but the flames have not as yet reached the second story. Again the lid of the mummy case is open an inch or so, but falls shut again. We hear the hammering of fists from inside the case—Mr. Walsh still survives.

---

300   CLOSEUP OF WALSH—Inside Case

He is yelling for help—desperate.

CUT TO:

301 EXTERIOR: Alleyway—Back of Museum

Showing workmen, the Cardiff Giant, and volunteer firemen leading out horses, zebras. Other people are wheeling out cages of roaring lions and tigers. (We must get over, all the animals are saved, for reasons of censorship.)

CUT TO:

302 INTERIOR: Barnum's American Museum— Medium Shot

Showing Barnum, his face now completely covered with grime and soot, leading out a camel. He is carrying a baby Shetland pony under one arm and has a monkey perched on his head. He staggers toward street. (This sort of scene is the cause of nervous breakdowns among directors.)

CUT TO:

303 EXTERIOR: Barnum's American Museum— Flashes

Showing firemen on ladders, swarming to the roof, playing the hose. A chief shouting through his trumpet to the men below. Some men up-and-downing at a windlass-pump.

304 CLOSE SHOT OF SKIFF AND A CONFEDERATE —
EXTERIOR: Barnum's American Museum

Skiff is looking on, triumphantly.

> SKIFF *to his aide:* Well, that's the end of Phineas Barnum!

> ANGRY VOICE *on* SOUND TRACK: OH, IT IS, IS IT!

CAMERA PULLS BACK to include the Bearded Lady who has just entered scene in time to overhear this remark. Most of her beard has been singed off. She is carrying a trunk, which she throws down, and before Skiff can move, she leaps upon him, bearing him to the ground. Skiff's confederate attempts to aid his chief, but the Bearded Lady lashes out with her heels, *à la savat*, and catches the confederate in the stomach. He doubles up, clasping his midriff and howling. The Bearded Lady is swarming over Skiff, who yammers and screeches. She reduces him to a pulp.

CUT TO:

---

305 EXTERIOR: Barnum's American Museum —
Close Shot

Barnum staggers out with another cargo of animals, turns them over to Tod and other workmen. At this moment the two terrified draymen who carried in the

Egyptian mummy case containing Mr. Walsh, rush up
to Barnum.

> FIRST DRAYMAN: There's a man inside....
> SECOND DRAYMAN *finishing for him:* ... In
> the mummy case ...
> BARNUM *bewildered—bellows:* WHAT!
> FIRST DRAYMAN *panicky:* A friend of yours
> —he said it was a joke, and ...
> BARNUM: What you talking about? ... A man!
> WHERE?

Barnum, Sam and the two workmen, run back into the
museum and are swallowed up in smoke.

CUT TO:

---

306   INTERIOR: Barnum's American Museum—
Medium Shot of Balcony on Second Floor

The smoke is thick now and the flames are licking
along the floor. The Egyptian mummy case can only
be glimpsed occasionally through the hot fog.

CUT TO:

---

307   CLOSEUP OF WALSH — Inside Case

He is fighting to get out—yelling and pounding madly
for help.

George Brasno (Tom Thumb), Tex Masden (Cardiff Giant), Wallace Beery (P. T. Barnum), Olive Brasno (Mrs. Tom Thumb), and Jolly Ethel (The Fat Lady).

308   INTERIOR: Barnum's American Museum—
(Shooting from Stairway to Floor Below)

The smoke and flames are thick on the lower floor.
Barnum, a shadowy figure in the haze, dodges in and
starts up the stairway, his head lowered like a charging
bull.

> SAM'S VOICE *from floor below:* Come back,
> Mr. Barnum! You'll be trapped!
> BARNUM *gasping and choking:* There's a man
> up here!

He plunges up the stairs and PAST CAMERA.

309   INTERIOR: Barnum's American Museum—
Balcony on Second Floor

Barnum comes stumbling through the smoke. He is
making for the Egyptian mummy case. He finds it. He
struggles with the heavy barrel on top of the case, leaping back as a tongue of flame sears him. Then he
grimly sets to his task again until the barrel crashes
to the floor, leaving Barnum almost done in.

310   INTERIOR: Barnum's American Museum—
Close Shot at Mummy Case

Barnum, sweaty and groggy, leans over the case, pulls
up the lid. The smoke is dense. Barnum reaches in to

shake the occupant, and drops to his knees in his frenzy.

BARNUM *frantically—shaking him:* Mister! ... Mister! Get up!

Then the unquenchable Mr. Walsh sits up groggily, and looks at Barnum. Barnum gasps, too astonished to speak. Walsh essays a debonair smile.

WALSH: This is a nice warm welcome for an old friend. . . .

BARNUM *pop-eyed:* Where'd YOU come from?

WALSH: From the mouth of Hell.

BARNUM *grimly:* You've got a round-trip ticket! With this, his fist shoots out and catches Walsh on the chin. Walsh, like a jack-in-the-box, collapses into the mummy case. Barnum slams down the cover, staggers to his feet.

BARNUM *continuing—raging:* I told you I'd get even some day!

He starts out of scene groggily.

---

311   INTERIOR: Barnum's American Museum— Longer Shot of Balcony on Second Floor (Showing Stairway in Foreground)

Barnum is staggering grimly toward the stairway from the balcony in background. Let Walsh die!

CUT TO:

312 INTERIOR: Barnum's American Museum—
Close Shot at Top of Stairway—Second
Floor

Barnum has reached the stairway and is about to fight
his way down, but his conscience is pricking him. He
gives up the moral battle, turns and dashes back into
the smoke toward Walsh.

313 INTERIOR: Barnum's American Museum—
Second Floor—Close Shot at Egyptian
Mummy Case

Barnum comes into scene, coughing and choking. He
is holding a handkerchief to his face. He reaches the
mummy case, hurls open the lid, and calls down to the
seemingly inert occupant.

BARNUM: Wake up! You can't die here, Mr.
Walsh! Much as it pains me, I gotta save you!
At this moment, Mr. Walsh's foot comes from the
depths of the mummy case and catches Barnum, *à la
savat*, squarely on the point of his chin. Barnum
gives a grunt and crumples to the floor. Walsh gets
out of the mummy case, dusting off his hands. As he
steps over the case, he glances down at the prostrate
Barnum.

WALSH: Foul me, will you? ... Let that be a lesson ...

He stalks with a weaving motion out of the scene.

CUT TO:

314 EXTERIOR: Barnum's American Museum — Flash — Close Shot of Nancy and Ellen

Nancy is struggling with a policeman, wild-eyed, distraught, fighting.

NANCY: Let me go to him! ... Phin-ee-as!

The policeman is having a hard time holding her back, with the help of Ellen.

CUT TO:

315 INTERIOR: Barnum's American Museum — Close Shot of Walsh on Stairway

Exhausted, Walsh staggers into scene and sinks on the stairway, shakes his head to clear it. Then he suddenly realizes what he has done. With great determination, he gets to his feet and starts back toward Barnum. He can't let his old pal pass out like this.

CUT TO:

316 INTERIOR: Barnum's American Museum— Medium Shot Upper Floor

Walsh teeters into scene, fumbling along. He locates a small fire bucket which hangs against the wall. With superhuman effort, he takes down the bucket and starts out, CAMERA FOLLOWING him as he stumbles through the haze. He stops, as he locates Barnum's prone form.

CUT TO:

317 INTERIOR: Barnum's American Museum— Upper Floor—Another Angle

Very deliberately, Walsh throws the contents of the pail into Barnum's face. This douche revives the great man. He gulps, splutters, makes swimming motions and sits up. Then he sees Walsh, and lurches to his feet, ready to fight.

WALSH *clinching him and holding him up:* Listen you big oaf! I couldn't let you burn to death without telling you about Jenny.

BARNUM: You can HAVE her! I don't even want to hear her name!

WALSH: You've got to listen, P. T. I DIDN'T MARRY MISS LIND. I haven't seen her but once since she left.

BARNUM: But you ran away with her!

229

WALSH: That's where you're wrong. We were fine friends. Nothing more. THAT'S WHAT I CAME BACK TO TELL YOU!
BARNUM *pushing himself back and saluting:* Jumpin' Jehosophat! Why didn't you say so before? I owe you an apology, Mr. Walsh ... You're one of Nature's princes. *They fall, through exhaustion and emotion, into each other's arms.*

---

318   INTERIOR: Barnum's American Museum — Second Floor

Barnum and Walsh suddenly become aware of the fire. Both take it big as the stairway sags. They look on aghast.

---

319   INTERIOR: Barnum's American Museum — Shooting from Second Floor to Lower Floor (From Their Angle)

With a resounding crash, the blazing stairway topples and falls to the inferno below. The whole first floor is sending up an impassable curtain of flame.

320 INTERIOR: Barnum's American Museum—
Second Floor—Medium Shot of Barnum and
Walsh

As they look down the burning hallway.
BARNUM: Jiminy Crickets! I'd plumb forgot
all about it!
WALSH *a game citizen, come what may:* Phineas,
would it offend you if I suggested a hasty depar-
ture?
Barnum gasps and points toward the window. The
space between them and the window is blurred with
smoke, a tongue of flame occasionally punctuating the
intervening space. They stumble toward the window.
CUT TO:

321 EXTERIOR: Barnum's American Museum—
Closeup of Nancy

She is still giving her police guardians (there are
three of them now) a battle—howbeit, a feeble one.
NANCY: If Phineas goes to his Maker, I want
to go with him! Leave me be!
Suddenly there is a shout on SOUND TRACK.
CROWD *ad libbing:*
There he is!
Hooray for Barnum!

It's Barnum and somebody else!
Dazed, Nancy looks up and off toward balcony, and sees—

---

322   CLOSE SHOT OF BARNUM AND WALSH ON BAL-
      CONY—(Shooting up)

They are just emerging to the balcony. The men are supporting each other. Smoke and flames are at their backs.

CUT TO:

---

323   CLOSEUP OF ELLEN

As she recognizes Walsh. Her eyes pop open—she holds her breath.

CUT TO:

---

324   EXTERIOR: Barnum's American Museum—
      Longer Shot

The crowd yells with frenzied encouragement, as several firemen rush to a spot under the balcony, spreading a large tarpaulin for a landing net.

CUT TO:

325   CLOSE SHOT OF BARNUM AND WALSH ON BAL-
       CONY

They are looking down at the net. On SOUND TRACK
we hear the crowd calling to them.
    CROWD *ad libbing:*
        Jump!
        The wall's giving way!
        Allez oup, Mr. Barnum!
    BARNUM: At my age, I gotta turn acrobat.
Come, Mr. Walsh, after you.
They jump; Walsh first, then Barnum.

                          CUT TO:

326   EXTERIOR: Street Ouside Barnum's American
       Museum – Flash

Showing the crowd, as the leapers sail through the air.
                          CUT TO:

327   CLOSE SHOT AT NET – EXTERIOR: Barnum's
       American Museum

As Walsh, and then Barnum land hard on the tarp.
Nancy, with a shriek, breaks loose from the policemen
and runs up to her spouse. Ellen follows.
    NANCY: Phin-ee-as! . . .

                          233

Then, seeing Walsh, she takes it big.

NANCY: Merciful Heavens! The bad penny's come back!

She is in a swooning mood. Ellen seizes her as she falls.

DISSOLVE TO:

---

328   EXTERIOR: Barnum's American Museum—
Long Shot Later on Same Night

Showing the smouldering ruins of Mr. Barnum's once-gaudy emporium. Everything is over. There is a funereal air about the ruin. Even the curiosity seekers have started to drift away.

CUT TO:

---

329   CLOSE SHOT OF A CARRIAGE — EXTERIOR:
Street

This is a nondescript vehicle, commandeered for the occasion. In it sits the forlorn and exhausted Nancy, and beside her is Ellen—happy withal, with dimpled romance singing in her heart. Madame Zorro, now a practically beardless lady, sits in the front seat with the driver.

NANCY *calling off:* It's 'most midnight, Phineas. . . . Watcha waitin' for? . . . It's all over.

CUT TO:

234

330 CLOSE SHOT OF BARNUM AND WALSH — EXTERIOR: Barnum's American Museum

Squatting side by side on the curbstone—world-weary figures to be sure. The charred hulk of the Museum is behind them.

BARNUM *once again dethroned:* You said it, Nancy.... It's all over....

331 EXTERIOR: Street Outside Museum

SHOT to include the two battered and fatigued gentlemen, and the women in the carriage. Nancy looks down at Barnum uneasily—he has been known to get up from the canvas before, with weird antics, long after the mob left him defeated and slug-nutty.

NANCY: I don't like to leave you two together. ...No tellin' WHAT'LL happen.

BARNUM: There isn't anything left to happen. Run along to the General's house like a good girl. I'll show up later.

Walsh and Ellen have been exchanging looks. He is smiling at her wearily.

ELLEN: Are you comin' too, Mr. Walsh?

WALSH: Nothing could keep me away, Ellen. This time I mean it....

Ellen flutters. The carriage starts out. Suddenly Barnum is struck by an idea, and gets to his feet, his knee-hinges creaking.

BARNUM *with a remnant of excitement:* Hey, Madame Zorro! How long before you can grow that beard again?

ZORRO: Three months—if I use tonic.

BARNUM *his enthusiasm drenched:* Nev' mind —there's no hurry.

He sits down again, as the carriage drives out of scene.

---

332 CLOSE SHOT OF BARNUM AND WALSH — EXTERIOR: Barnum's American Museum

---

They are still sitting alone on the curbstone, both staring into space. Barnum's expression is hopeless. At this moment we hear, faintly, the sound of a band. It comes closer and closer—a brisk, marching air. There are shouts. Walsh looks up as though suddenly remembering something. Barnum's tired head snaps up with a jerk. He looks off in the direction of the music.

---

333 EXTERIOR: Street (Shooting from Barnum's Angle) — Medium Shot

---

Coming toward Barnum and Walsh, is a band, the procession lighted by torches. And—marching along with majestic tread is a huge elephant. A group of kids are following and yelling. People are stopping at the curb to gape, coming out of houses, peering out of windows.

---

334   CLOSE SHOT OF BARNUM AND WALSH — EXTERIOR: Barnum's American Museum

---

Barnum is staring off, his eyes bulging, at the parade. The sound of music comes closer. Barnum half raises himself from the curb, awed beyond measure. He rubs his eyes, then gives another "take 'em."

BARNUM: Jumpin' Jehosophat, and all the ten graces! It—it CAN'T be! No!

WALSH: It is, though, Phineas. It's JUMBO, direct from England.

BARNUM *on his feet, and ready to die of chagrin:* Mr. Walsh, there goes my life ambition—and what's worst, I know where it's going—to Skiff's Canal Street Museum! . . . the varmint!

WALSH *getting to his feet and stretching:* Oh no, my friend—yonder Jumbo belongs to none other than P. T. Barnum— It's yours—a gift!

BARNUM *speechless:* A gift! FROM WHO?

WALSH: From Jenny Lind.

BARNUM: Stop jokin' with a dying man. . . . *He is so nervous that his suspenders break.*

WALSH *interrupting:* Hold everything, Phineas. . . . *Barnum makes a dive to rescue his drooping garment:* . . . She bought Jumbo—as an atonement present. She's always regretted the way she deserted you—her impresario.

BARNUM: She's a lady, Mr. Walsh—a REAL lady! But shucks, I'm no impresario. I'm a SHOW-MAN! *Suddenly remembers Jumbo—the czar again:* Come on! What're we standin' here for? There's JUMBO! ... JUMBO, the blessed angel straight from Heaven!

DISSOLVE TO:

335   EXTERIOR: Street—Close Trucking Shot of Jumbo

Jumbo is marching majestically along the street, lighted flares illuminating the parade. On SOUND TRACK we hear the band playing.

CUT TO:

336   EXTERIOR: Street—Close Trucking Shot of Barnum and Walsh

They are striding ahead of the band, with Jumbo leading the parade. Barnum is marching proudly, bowing right and left. Walsh is beside him. On SOUND TRACK we hear the cheers of people. The neighborhood has turned out *en masse*.

BARNUM *bowing to the onlookers:* Sir, to you!

238

Jumbo, the King of elephants! *To Walsh:* He's wuth his weight in gold, Mr. Walsh! ... Wait'll I exhibit him! We'll make a fortune!

WALSH: Exhibit him! WHERE? In a vacant lot? For the moment Barnum is stumped. Then his face lights up.

BARNUM: Why not? In a barn, or a tent—or something. ... *Appalled by his own talents:* Mr. Walsh! That gives me an idea! Why don't we have a big tent made? Big enough to hold all the animals, freaks and—don't you see? When business got bad, we could move the whole shebang from place to place.

WALSH: Phineas, you're a genius.

BARNUM *endeavoring to be a shrinking violet:* You're just as big a genius. In fact, we're both GENIUSES! We oughta go in partnership. With big signs—"BARNUM & WALSH" ... *He frowns:* That don't rhyme, somehow. ... *Walsh subdues a smile.* Say, I've often wondered. What's your FIRST name?

WALSH *with a grin:* It's a family secret. My first name is BAILEY.

BARNUM: Bailey! ... Bailey! That's got it— Barnum and Bailey. It rhymes. SHAKE, pardner! They shake hands while walking. Barnum's eyes are filled with soot and dreams. The band plays more loudly.

BARNUM *continuing:* You know, you never can

239

tell—people are liable to be talkin' about us one hundred years from now—BARNUM AND BAILEY! THE GREATEST SHOW ON EARTH!

DISSOLVE TO:

---

337   EXTERIOR: Circus Tents – Medium Shot – Day

This is a modern scene, as in first scene of picture, showing the sign: "BARNUM & BAILEY—THE GREATEST SHOW ON EARTH."

We pick up the routine shown in first scene of picture, at the point where we left it. The act finishes.

QUICK MONTAGE SHOTS of people crowding into the great tents. We hear the triumphant blast from a calliope. A band is playing. Barkers' voices in a blur:— "Right this way, to the big tent—performance just starting—The greatest show on earth. . . ."

And in this medley of sound and confusion of color, we

FADE OUT.